EMILY DICKINSON

Recent Titles in Greenwood Biographies

J.K. Rowling: A Biography
Connie Ann Kirk

The Dalai Lama: A Biography
Patricia Cronin Marcello

Margaret Mead: A Biography
Mary Bowman-Kruhm

J.R.R. Tolkien: A Biography
Leslie Ellen Jones

Colin Powell: A Biography
Richard Steins

Pope John Paul II: A Biography
Meg Greene

Al Capone: A Biography
Luciano Iorizzo

George S. Patton: A Biography
David A. Smith

Gloria Steinem: A Biography
Patricia Cronin Marcello

Billy Graham: A Biography
Roger Bruns

EMILY DICKINSON

A Biography

Connie Ann Kirk

GREENWOOD BIOGRAPHIES

GREENWOOD PRESS
WESTPORT, CONNECTICUT · LONDON

Library of Congress Cataloging-in-Publication Data

Kirk, Connie Ann.
    Emily Dickinson : a biography / Connie Ann Kirk.
        p. cm.—(Greenwood biographies, ISSN 1540–4900)
    Includes bibliographical references (p.) and index.
    ISBN 0–313–32206–6 (alk. paper)
    1. Dickinson, Emily, 1830–1886. 2. Poets, American—19th century—Biography.
3. Amherst (Mass.)—Biography. I. Title. II. Series.
PS1541.Z5K588 2004
811′.4—dc22
[B]   2003058335

British Library Cataloguing in Publication Data is available.

Library of Congress Catalog Card Number: 2003058335

ISBN: 0–313–32206–6
ISSN: 1540–4900

First published in 2004

Greenwood Press, 88 Post Road West, Westport, CT 06881
An imprint of Greenwood Publishing Group, Inc.
www.greenwood.com

Printed in the United States of America

The paper used in this book complies with the
Permanent Paper Standard issued by the National
Information Standards Organization (Z39.48–1984).

10 9 8 7 6 5 4 3 2 1

Copyright Acknowledgments

Reprinted by permission of the publishers and the Trustees of Amherst College from
THE POEMS OF EMILY DICKINSON: READING EDITION, Ralph W. Franklin,
ed., Cambridge, Mass.: The Belknap Press of Harvard University Press, Copyright © 1998
by the President and Fellows of Harvard College. Copyright © 1951, 1955, 1979, by
the President and Fellows of Harvard College.

Reprinted by permission of the publishers from THE LETTERS OF EMILY DICKINSON,
Thomas H. Johnson, ed., Cambridge, Mass.: The Belknap Press of Harvard University
Press, Copyright © 1958, 1986 by the President and Fellows of Harvard College.

Every reasonable effort has been made to trace the owners of copyright materials in this
book, but in some instances this has proven impossible. The author and publisher will be
glad to receive information leading to more complete acknowledgments in subsequent
printings of the book and in the meantime extend their apologies for any omissions.

In honor of my beloved parents,
Leonard A. Lewis and Mary Arlene Lewis,
married, so far, 60 years.
They made home a holy word.

CONTENTS

Appendixes

Photo essay follows page 76

SERIES FOREWORD

In response to high school and public library needs, Greenwood developed this distinguished series of full-length biographies specifically for student use. Prepared by field experts and professionals, these engaging biographies are tailored for high school students who need challenging yet accessible biographies. Ideal for secondary school assignments, the length, format, and subject areas are designed to meet educators' requirements and students' interests.

Greenwood offers an extensive selection of biographies spanning all curriculum related subject areas including social studies, the sciences, literature and the arts, history and politics, as well as popular culture, covering public figures and famous personalities from all time periods and backgrounds, both historic and contemporary, who have made an impact on American and/or world culture. Greenwood biographies were chosen based on comprehensive feedback from librarians and educators. Consideration was given to both curriculum relevance and inherent interest. The result is an intriguing mix of the well known and the unexpected, the saints and sinners from long-ago history and contemporary pop culture. Readers will find a wide array of subject choices from fascinating crime figures like Al Capone to inspiring pioneers like Margaret Mead, from the greatest minds of our time like Stephen Hawking to the most amazing success stories of our day like J. K. Rowling.

While the emphasis is on fact, not glorification, the books are meant to be fun to read. Each volume provides in-depth information about the subject's life from birth through childhood, the teen years, and adulthood. A thorough account relates family background and education, traces personal and professional influences, and explores struggles, accomplishments, and contributions. A timeline highlights the most significant life events against a historical perspective. Bibliographies supplement the reference value of each volume.

PREFACE

I'm not quite sure when my relationship with Emily Dickinson began, but I know I read a smattering of her work before college. I had written about her in a Dickinson graduate seminar as well as in my dissertation. I had visited her home and taught her works for several years at the college level, but it was not until 1999, when I attended my first Dickinson conference at Mount Holyoke, that I became a member of her "select Society" for good. Since that time, and with the warm friendships and collegiality I have enjoyed as a member of the Emily Dickinson International Society (EDIS), I have taught Dickinson to a global community of learners over the Internet, edited a Dickinson Internet discussion group (with subscribers from over a dozen countries), written and presented academic papers on the poet and the poems internationally, gingerly handled original Dickinson manuscripts and family papers at important holdings at Harvard and Brown Universities and elsewhere, and worked inside the cool, shadowy rooms of The Evergreens as it continues to undergo restoration.

This book is part of Greenwood's biography series for which I have written before. This time, however, the opportunity to write a biography of approximately 200 manuscript pages for young people about a subject for whom I have so much affection and admiration is both an honor and a special responsibility. Anyone familiar with Dickinson scholarship knows that the biography is a particularly touchy subject—it has been done badly so many times before, and the mythology surrounding the poet is a living, breathing enterprise unto itself. However, my belief is that young adults may not take the time to read the excellent, full-scale literary biographies available. That they should, nonetheless, have the opportunity to be exposed to current and accurate information about the poet fueled my efforts. The support of "Emfriends," most of whom are members of the Emily Dickinson International Society, kept moving me, one foot in front of the other, when my path grew uncertain.

For this project, I would like to thank Lynn Araujo of Greenwood who asked me to write the book, then remained patient with me as I nudged deadlines steadily backward for the sole purpose of gathering more primary research that was not necessary for an educational series such as this one. I would like to thank the Director of the Emily Dickinson Museum, Cindy Dickinson, and Assistant Director, Jane Wald, for their support, answers to my many questions, and generous access to both houses. Thanks also go to Leslie Morris and Susan Halpert of the Houghton Library at Harvard University; Mark Brown of the John Hay Library at Brown University; and the staff of Special Collections at Amherst College and the Jones Library.

Special thanks for their intelligence, generosity, support, and ongoing friendship, whether they contributed knowledge to this particular project or to other research I have ongoing in Dickinson, go to fellow Dickinson scholars, Betty Bernhard, Jane Eberwein, Margaret H. Freeman, Cindy MacKenzie, Martha Nell Smith, Georgiana Strickland, and Marcy Tanter—"Emfriends," all. Discussions with Jerry Liebling, Polly Longsworth, and so many others, as well as the many fine conference papers I have heard over the years also contributed to this project. Lastly, I thank my dear family—Ken, Ben, and John for their enduring love, good humor, and support, and for allowing me to be at home with Emily Dickinson, and glad.

TIMELINE: CHRONOLOGY & HISTORICAL CONTEXT

Historical/cultural events appear in bold type.

1620 Dec. 11 **Plymouth Colony is established by Mayflower pilgrims who sign the Mayflower Compact.**

c. 1637 Puritans Nathaniel and Ann Gull Dickinson emigrate from Lincolnshire, England, to British outpost at Wethersfield, Connecticut.

1659 Nathaniel and Ann Dickinson and their children move north and help establish the town of Hadley, Massachusetts.

1754 **French and Indian War begins. Lasts until 1763.**

1759 Town of Amherst, Massachusetts, is established out of eastern portion of Hadley.

1770 **Mar. 5** **Boston Massacre.**

1773 **Dec. 16** **Boston Tea Party.**

1775 **Apr. 19** **Battle of Lexington and Concord (50 miles from Amherst) begins the Revolutionary War.**

1776 Joel Norcross, Emily's maternal grandfather, is born in Sturbridge, Massachusetts.

July 4 **Americans declare independence from Great Britain.**

Oct. 9 Samuel Fowler Dickinson, Emily's paternal grandfather, is born.

1777 William Norcross and Sarah Marsh Norcross, Emily's maternal great grandparents, move to Monson, Massachusetts.

Betsey Fay (Norcross) is born.

1783	Sept. 3	Treaty of Paris is signed by Britain and the United States, ending the Revolutionary War.
1788	Feb. 6	Massachusetts is the sixth state to ratify the U.S. Constitution.
		Sarah Vaill (Norcross) is born.
1789	Apr. 30	George Washington is sworn in as the first president of the United States.
1791	Dec. 15	Bill of Rights ratified (first 10 Amendments to the U.S. Constitution).
1794		Eli Whitney patents the cotton gin.
1800	Dec. 12	Washington, D.C. becomes the nation's official capital.
1801	Mar. 4	Thomas Jefferson is sworn in as the third president of the United States.
1803		William Norcross, Emily's maternal great grandfather, dies.
	Jan. 1	Edward Dickinson, Emily's father, is born.
	Apr. 30	United States makes the Louisiana Purchase.
1804	May 17	Lewis and Clark Expedition begins.
	July 3	Emily Norcross (Dickinson), Emily's mother, is born.
1806		Monson Academy is founded.
1807		Robert Fulton sails the first steamboat, *Clermont*, from New York to Albany.
1812	June 11	The United States declares war on Britain, beginning the War of 1812.
		Lavinia Norcross (Norcross) is born.
1813		Samuel Fowler Dickinson builds the Homestead, the first brick house in Amherst.
1814		Amherst Academy is founded.
	Aug. 24	The British set fire to Washington, D.C.
	Sept. 20	"Star-Spangled Banner" becomes the official national anthem.
1821		Amherst College is founded.
1823		Thomas Wentworth Higginson is born.
	Dec. 2	In an address to Congress, President Monroe declares the Monroe Doctrine prohibiting further European colonization in the Americas.
1825	Oct. 26	Erie Canal opens.
1828	May 6	Emily Norcross and Edward Dickinson marry.
		Emily Lavinia Norcross, the poet's cousin, is born.
1829	Mar. 24	Andrew Jackson is sworn in as seventh president of the United States.

	Apr. 16	William Austin Dickinson, Emily's brother, is born.
1830	Apr. 3	Edward Dickinson buys west half of the Homestead.
	Oct. 14	Helen Fiske (Hunt Jackson) is born.
	Dec. 10	EMILY ELIZABETH DICKINSON is born at the Homestead.
	Dec. 19	Susan Huntington Gilbert is born in Deerfield, Massachusetts.
1833		**First sewing machine invented.**
	Feb. 28	Lavinia Norcross Dickinson, the poet's sister, is born.
	Mar.	S. F. Dickinson sells his half of the Homestead to Gen. David Mack; moves to Cincinnati.
	Mar. 4	**Andrew Jackson is sworn in for a second term as president of the United States.**
	May–June	2-year-old Emily visits Aunt Lavinia Norcross for an extended visit in Monson.
1835	Feb. 28	Edward Dickinson is appointed Amherst College treasurer.
	Sept. 7	Emily begins education at West Center District School.
1836		**Samuel Colt develops the 6-shooter revolver.**
	Feb.–Mar.	**Texans defend the Alamo against Mexican invaders.**
1838	Jan.	Edward Dickinson begins first term in Massachusetts State Legislature.
	Apr. 22	S. F. Dickinson dies in Hudson, Ohio.
1840	Apr.	Edward Dickinson sells his half of the Homestead to Gen. Mack and the family moves to West Street house (now North Pleasant Street).
	Sept. 7	Emily and Lavinia begin Amherst Academy.
1842		**Ether anesthesia first used in an operation by Crawford Williamson Long, of Georgia.**
	April	Austin begins Williston Seminary. Emily writes first extant letter (to Austin).
		Louisa (Loo) Norcross is born.
1844		**Samuel F. B. Morse demonstrates his telegraph by sending a message from Washington, D.C. to Baltimore.**
	Apr. 29	Sophia Holland dies.
	May	Emily Dickinson visits Aunt Lavinia in Boston and Uncle William in Worcester to recuperate from emotional trauma of Sophia Holland's death.
	June	Emily meets new student, Abiah Root, on Amherst Academy stairway.

	Dec.	Religious revivals hit Amherst. Emily does not attend.
1845	Feb.	Abiah Root leaves Amherst Academy; Emily begins writing letters to her.
	Apr. 15	Edward Hitchcock becomes president of Amherst College.
1846		**Cylinder printing press is developed by Richard M. Hoe.**
	May 5	Joel Norcross, the poet's maternal grandfather, dies.
	May 13	**The United States declares war on Mexico.**
	Aug. 25	Emily visits Boston again for her health.
	Aug.	Austin begins Amherst College.
	Nov. 12	Father serves as chairman at Amherst Cattle Show.
1847	early	Emily sits for famous daguerreotype.
	Aug. 4	Frances Lavinia (Fanny) Norcross, cousin, is born.
	Aug. 10	Emily completes last year at Amherst Academy.
	Aug.	Abiah Root visits Amherst.
	Sept. 30	Emily begins school at Mount Holyoke.
	Oct. 16	Austin, Vinnie, and Abby Wood visit Emily at Mount Holyoke.
	Nov. 3	Mother and Father visit Emily at Mount Holyoke.
	Nov. 24 –29	Emily home in Amherst for Thanksgiving break.
1848	Jan. 21– Feb. 7	Emily home in Amherst on winter break from Mount Holyoke.
	Jan. 24	**Gold is discovered at Sutter's Mill, initiating the California Gold Rush.**
	Mar. 25– May 11	Emily home on spring break from Mount Holyoke and is also ill.
	Aug.	Emily's last session at Mount Holyoke. Father decides not to send her another year.
	July 19–20	**Seneca Falls Women's Rights Convention is held, Seneca Falls, New York, 10 miles from Geneva.**
	Aug. 3	Abiah Root attends Mount Holyoke commencement but does not speak to Emily.
	Oct. 29	Emily writes Abiah Root about their dwindling friendship.
	Dec. 19	Emily Brontë (one of Emily's favorite poets) dies.
1849	Mar. 5	Mary Lyon (founder of Mount Holyoke) dies.

	May	Austin brings home the new book, *Kavanagh* by Longfellow.
	Aug.	Benjamin Newton leaves Amherst.
	Oct. 9	Emily, Vinnie, and friends climb Mt. Holyoke.
	Dec. 5	Vinnie begins Ipswich Seminary.
	Dec. 6	**Harriet Tubman escapes from slavery on the Underground Railroad.**
1850	Jan.	Benjamin Newton sends Emily Emerson's *Poems* (published in 1847).
	Jan.	Father brings home a Newfoundland to accompany Emily on her walks.
	Late Feb.	Emily's "Magnum bonum" valentine is published in Amherst College *Indicator*. Carlo is mentioned as Emily's dog's name for the first time.
	Mar.–Aug.	More religious revivals in Amherst. Emily still resists.
	c. spring	Austin and Susan begin their secret courtship. Emily and Susan are also close friends and talk about books and writing.
	c. May 5	Emily refuses to go on a ride with George Gould, saying she must stay home to take care of her ill mother.
	Aug. 8	Austin graduates from Amherst College.
	Aug. 11	Both Father and Susan Gilbert profess their faith at a revival and join First Church.
	Sept.	Austin begins teaching at Sunderland. He and Susan have a secret pact to eat a chestnut every evening at the same time in remembrance of one another.
	Sept. 9	**California is admitted to the Union as the thirty-first state.**
	Nov. 3	Vinnie professes faith and joins First Church.
1851	Jan. 1	Vinnie begins diary.
	June 4	Benjamin Newton marries.
	June 7	Austin begins teaching at Endicott School in Boston.
	July 3	Jenny Lind recital in Northampton attended by Emily and her family.
	July 26	Bad fire in Amherst in which Father is helpful and the town is grateful.
	Sept. 6–22	Emily and Vinnie visit Austin in Boston and stay with Aunt Lavinia.
	Sept.	Susan goes to Baltimore to teach mathematics at Archer's School for Young Ladies.

	Sept. 29	Father sees the aurora borealis and rings the church bell so that the townspeople won't miss seeing it.
1852		**Harriet Beecher Stowe's _Uncle Tom's Cabin_ is published.**
	Feb. 20	Emily's "Sic transit Gloria mund" valentine is published in the _Springfield Republican_.
	June	Father visits Susan in Baltimore during Whig Convention.
	July 26	Austin finishes teaching and arrives back in Amherst.
	Dec. 17	Father is elected Representative of Tenth District of Massachusetts for the United States Congress.
1853	Mar. 9	Austin begins Harvard Law School.
	Mar. 23	Susan visits Austin in Boston at the Revere House Hotel; they become engaged.
	Mar. 24	Benjamin Newton dies at age 32.
	Mar. 27	Emily's letter to Austin relates that she is writing.
	May 9	Amherst-Belchertown Railroad line opens.
	June 9	"New London Day" for the A&B Railroad
	c. early Sept.	Emily and Vinnie visit the Hollands in Springfield.
	Dec. 5	Father attends Thirty-third Congress of the United States.
1854	Mar. 31	Charlotte Brontë (author of _Jane Eyre_, which Emily read) dies.
	Apr.	Mother, Vinnie, and Austin visit Father in Washington, D.C. Emily stays at the Homestead with Susan Gilbert and John Graves.
	July 19	Austin graduates from Harvard Law School.
	Sept. 19 –20	Emily and Vinnie make a second visit to the Hollands in Springfield.
1855	c. Feb.–Mar.	Emily and Vinnie visit Father in Washington, D.C.
	c. Mar. 4	Emily and Vinnie go to Philadelphia on their way home from Washington, D.C. and stay with Eliza Coleman. Emily may have heard Rev. Charles Wadsworth preach at the Arch Street Presbyterian Church.
	Apr.	Father buys back all of the Homestead from Gen. Mack.
	Aug. 8	Ralph Waldo Emerson makes address at Amherst College commencement.

	Oct. 31	Father and Austin form law partnership. Renovations on the Homestead are nearly completed.
	Nov. 6	Father is defeated in his run for Congress as the Whig Party candidate.
	mid-Nov.	Father, Mother, Austin, Emily, and Vinnie all move to the Homestead.
1856	Jan. 6	Austin professes faith and joins the First Church, probably due to Susan's influence.
	July 1	Austin and Susan are married in Geneva, New York; they take up residence in The Evergreens next door to the Homestead.
	Oct. 17	Emily's bread wins second prize at the Agricultural Fair.
	c. Oct.	Norcross cousins visit the Homestead.
1857	**Feb.**	**Supreme Court rules in Dred Scott case, forbidding Congress from banning slavery in states and deciding that slaves are not citizens.**
	Aug. 28	Emily on Cattle Show committee, makes rye and Indian bread.
	Dec. 16	Emerson lectures in Amherst on "The Beautiful in Rural Life" and stays at The Evergreens.
1858		Emily begins assembling her poems into portfolios.
	c. spring	Emily writes first "Master" letter.
	Aug.–Oct.	**Lincoln–Douglas debates for Illinois state election campaign bring Lincoln national attention.**
	Oct.	Clara and Anna Newman, cousins, live at The Evergreens as wards of Edward Dickinson.
1859		**Oil strike in Titusville, Pennsylvania, results in world's first oil boom.**
	Jan.	Emily writes first extant letter to cousin Louise Norcross.
	Mar.	Father walks Emily home after late-night party at The Evergreens.
	Oct. 16	**John Brown Revolt in the cause of abolition.**
1860		**Winchester repeating rifle developed.**
	mid-Mar.	Charles Wadsworth visits Emily in Amherst.
	Apr. 17	Aunt Lavinia Norcross Norcross dies.
	June 9	Judge Lord and his wife visit the Homestead.
	Aug.	Helen Fiske Hunt (later named Helen Hunt Jackson) and her husband, Major Hunt, visit the Homestead.

	Oct.	Emily and Vinnie visit Eliza Coleman in Middletown.
	Nov. 6	**Abraham Lincoln elected president of the United States.**
	Dec. 20	**South Carolina secedes from the Union.**
1861	c. Jan.	The poet writes second "Master" letter.
		South secedes from the Union.
	Mar. 4	**Abraham Lincoln is inaugurated as president of the United States.**
	Apr. 12	**First shots of the Civil War are fired at Fort Sumter, South Carolina.**
	May 4, 11	Emily's "I taste a liquor never brewed - ", is published anonymously in the *Springfield Republican*, under the title, "The May Wine," presumably without her permission.
	June 19	Edward (Ned) Dickinson, nephew, is born. He is Austin and Susan's first child.
	June 20	**West Virginia becomes a state after refusing to secede from the Union with Virginia.**
	June 29	Elizabeth Barrett Browning (a favorite poet of Emily's) dies.
	July	**First Battle of Bull Run in Virginia.**
	c. Dec.	Emily seeks Susan's advice on the poem, "Safe in their Alabaster Chambers."
1862	early	Emily writes third "Master" letter.
	Mar. 1	Emily's "Safe in their Alabaster Chambers" appears anonymously in the *Springfield Republican* under the title, "The Sleeping." Another, possibly by Susan Dickinson, "The Shadow of Thy Wing" was printed underneath it.
	Mar. 14	Frazar Stearns from Amherst killed in action in Battle at Newburn, North Carolina.
	Apr.	Thomas Wentworth Higginson's "Letter to a Young Republican" appears in *The Atlantic Monthly*.
	Apr. 15	Emily writes to Higginson for the first time, enclosing four poems for his critique.
	Apr. 25	Emily writes second letter to Higginson and encloses three more poems.
	May 1	Charles Wadsworth and his family sail for San Francisco.
	May 6	Henry David Thoreau dies in Concord. *Walden* was in the Dickinson library.

	June 7	Emily writes third letter to Higginson, asking him to be her "preceptor."
	July 9	Judge Lord delivers Amherst commencement address.
	mid-July	Emily writes fourth letter to Higginson, enclosing four poems.
	Aug.	Emily sends fifth letter to Higginson, with two poems.
	Dec. 4	Higginson, a noted abolitionist, is appointed colonel of the black Twenty-Ninth regiment of the First South Carolina Volunteers in the Union Army.
1863	**Jan. 1**	**Lincoln issues Emancipation Proclamation freeing slaves in Confederate states.**
	Jan. 1	**Homestead Act enacted. Settlers could have up to 160 acres of free western land if they stayed on it and maintained it for five years.**
	Jan. 17	Uncle Loring Norcross (Aunt Lavinia's husband) dies, making Fanny and Loo orphans.
	Jul. 1–3	**Battle of Gettysburg in Pennsylvania causes Civil War's greatest number of dead, wounded, and captured soldiers in a single battle, about 50,000.**
	July 9	Father awarded L. L. D. at Amherst College.
	Oct. 1	Helen Hunt (Jackson's) husband, Major E. B. Hunt, is killed in Brooklyn.
	Nov. 19	**Lincoln delivers Gettysburg Address dedicating the battlefield as a national cemetery.**
1864	Feb. 27	Prof. Edward Hitchcock of Amherst College dies.
	Mar. 12	Emily's "Some keep the Sabbath going to church - " is published anonymously in *Round Table*.
	Mar. 30	Emily's "Blazing in Gold - and" appears anonymously in *Springfield Republican*.
	April	Emily travels to Cambridge, Massachusetts, for eye treatments.
	May 13	Austin pays $500 for an Irish substitute when he is drafted to serve in the Union army.
	May 19	**Nathaniel Hawthorne dies.**
	Nov. 28	Emily returns to Amherst from her eye treatment in Cambridge.
1865		**William Bullock introduces web-offset printing press that prints both sides of the paper at once; makes all previous printing presses obsolete.**
	Apr.	Emily goes back to Cambridge for second bout of eye treatments.

	Apr. 9	General Robert E. Lee surrenders to General Ulysses S. Grant at Appomattox Courthouse, Virginia, ending the Civil War.
	Apr. 14	**Abraham Lincoln is assassinated at Ford's Theater by John Wilkes Booth.**
	May 10	**Confederacy president, Jefferson Davis, is captured.**
	mid-May	Emily writes of "Jeff" Davis's capture in letter to Vinnie.
	Oct.	Emily returns to Amherst from Cambridge.
	Oct. 17	Emerson lectures in Amherst on "Social Aims."
	Dec. 6	**Thirteenth Amendment to the Constitution is enacted abolishing slavery.**
1866	Jan. 27	Carlo, Emily's Newfoundland and faithful companion of 16 years, dies.
	Feb. 14, 17	Emily's "A narrow Fellow in / the grass" appears in the *Springfield Republican*.
	Nov. 29	Martha Gilbert Dickinson, niece, is born.
1867		**Barbed wire invented by Lucien B. Smith of Ohio.**
1868	Sept. 23	Father dedicates new church that Austin supervised building.
1869	**May 10**	**Central Pacific and Union Pacific Railroads are joined at Promontory, Utah, creating the first transcontinental railroad.**
	May 11	Emily writes to Higginson that she cannot visit him in Boston because she does not cross her "Father's ground to any House or town."
1870		**Pneumatic subway is built underneath Broadway in New York City by Alfred Ely Beach.**
	Aug. 16	Higginson and Emily's famous first meeting at the Homestead.
1871		George Eliot's *Middlemarch* published. (Emily praises).
	Oct. 8–9	**Chicago's "Great Fire" kills 300 and leaves 90,000 people homeless.**
1872	July 10	Father resigns as Amherst College treasurer.
	mid-Oct.	Emily Fowler Ford's *My Recreations* is published.
1873		**Typewriter invented by Christopher Latham Sholes.**
	Dec. 1	Austin is elected to succeed his father as treasurer of Amherst College.
	Dec. 3	Higginson lectures in Amherst and visits Emily for a second time.

1874		**William Blackstone invents home washing machine.**
	June 16	Father dies from a sudden illness while giving a speech in Boston.
1875	June 15	Mother becomes paralyzed.
	Aug. 1	Thomas Gilbert (Gib) Dickinson, nephew, is born at The Evergreens.
	Oct. 22	Helen Fiske Hunt marries W. S. Jackson.
	Dec.	Judge Lord rises to Supreme Court of Massachusetts.
1876		**Alexander Graham Bell patents the telephone.**
	Mar. 20	Letter from Helen Hunt tells Emily she is wrong not to "sing aloud."
	June 25	**"Custer's Last Stand" at Little Big Horn. Lt. Col. George A. Custer is defeated by the Sioux led by Sitting Bull at the Little Big Horn River, Montana.**
	Aug. 20	Letter from Helen Hunt Jackson asks Emily for a poem to publish anonymously in Roberts Brothers' No Name Series, *Masque of Poets*.
	Oct.	Judge Lord and his wife visit the Homestead.
	Oct.–Nov.	Austin ill with malaria.
	Dec. 26	Susan gives Emily *Of the Imitation of Christ* by Thomas á Kempis.
1877		**Thomas Alva Edison invents the phonograph. The first telephone line is built from Boston to Somerville, Massachusetts.**
	June 28	Samuel Bowles visits Emily and demands that the "rascal" come down the stairway at once.
	Sept. 2	Mary Higginson dies.
	Oct.	Samuel Bowles is ill.
	Dec. 10	Mrs. Lord dies.
1878	Jan. 16	Samuel Bowles dies.
	Jan. 19	Austin and Vinnie attend Samuel Bowles's funeral.
	Apr. 29	Helen Hunt Jackson again asks Emily for her permission to publish poems.
	late June	Mother breaks her hip.
	Oct. 24	Helen Hunt Jackson and her husband visit Emily.
	Nov. 20	Emily's "Success is counted sweetest" is printed in *A Masque of Poets*.
	Dec. 10	"Success is counted sweetest" is erroneously attributed to Ralph Waldo Emerson.
1879		**Thomas Alva Edison invents the incandescent light bulb. James Ritty invents the cash register.**

	c. mid-Jan.	Emily receives her copy of *A Masque of Poets* from editor Thomas Niles of Roberts Brothers.
	Mar. 19	Ralph Waldo Emerson lectures again in Amherst.
	July 3–4	Largest fire in Amherst. Vinnie tells Emily that it is only fireworks, but maid Margaret Maher tells her the truth.
1880	Mar.	Austin ill again with malaria.
	c. early Aug.	Charles Wadsworth pays an unexpected visit.
	Aug. 23–30	Judge Lord visits Homestead again with his family.
	Sept. 23	Judge Lord visits Homestead with niece, Abby Farley.
	Sept. 26	Judge Lord visits Homestead again.
	mid-Nov.	Emily writes to Higginson about poems requested of her for charity.
	Dec. 24	George Eliot dies.
	Dec. 25	Judge Lord gives Emily the *Complete Concordance to Shakespeare*. She receives *Endymion* by Disraeli from Susan.
1881	Mar. 15	Judge Lord falls ill.
	Apr. 17	Judge Lord stays at The Evergreens as a guest; he is recovered.
	July 2	**President Garfield is shot.**
	Aug. 31	Professor David Peck Todd and Mabel Loomis Todd arrive in Amherst. Todd will teach astronomy at Amherst College.
	Oct. 12	Dr. Holland dies.
1882	Apr. 1	Charles Wadsworth dies.
	Apr. 16	Judge Lord visits Emily.
	Apr. 24	Thomas Niles encourages Emily to print poems.
	Apr. 27	Ralph Waldo Emerson dies.
	May 1	Judge Lord is very ill.
	July 15	Emily refuses to see Emily Fowler Ford.
	Sept. 10	Mabel Loomis Todd sings for Emily.
	Sept. 11	Mabel and Austin convey their affection for one another.
	Nov. 14	Dickinson's Mother dies.
1883	Aug. 8–9	Dickinson family reunion held in College Hall. Stage is decorated with wreaths, garlands, flags, guns, and family portraits. Up to 1,500 relatives were expected.
	Sept. 8	Judge Lord visits again.

Oct. 5	Gib dies after contracting typhoid fever while playing in the Amherst Common. Emily is diagnosed with "nervous prostration."
Oct. 7	Austin ill again with malaria.
Oct. 12	Vinnie also becomes ill.
Dec. 7	Matthew Arnold gives lecture in Amherst.
1884	**Riders board the first rollercoaster at Coney Island, New York, called the "Switchback."**
Mar. 13	Judge Lord dies.
Jun. 14	Emily passes out while baking a cake with Margaret Maher.
Sept. 5	Helen Hunt Jackson offers to be Emily's literary executor; the poet ignores her request.
1885	**First skyscraper, the 10-story Home Insurance Company building, is built using steel girders in Chicago.**
late Mar.	Emily writes to Helen Hunt Jackson, ignoring her offer to be Emily's literary executor.
Aug. 12	Helen Fiske Hunt Jackson dies.
1886 Jan. 12	Emily becomes very ill in the afternoon.
c. spring	Emily writes last letter to Higginson, telling him she has been too ill to read or think.
Mar. 18	Austin sits with Emily at her sickbed.
Mar. 24	Austin sits again with Emily at her sickbed.
c. early May	Emily writes "Called back" letter to Norcross cousins.
May 13	Emily loses consciousness.
May 15	EMILY ELIZABETH DICKINSON dies at the Homestead, just before the whistles sound for 6 p.m.
May 19	The poet's funeral is held at the Homestead. Higginson reads Emily Brontë's "No coward soul."
Oct. 28	**Statue of Liberty is dedicated in New York Harbor.** Susan begins working on edition of Emily's poems.
1887	**Platter-design record is developed for the phonograph by Emile Berliner.**
1888	Vinnie retrieves poems from Susan and gives some to Mabel Loomis Todd to edit.
	George Eastman develops the first Kodak camera in Rochester, New York, which features a 100-exposure roll of film that is developed by the manufacturer after the photographer shoots the pictures.

1890 Nov. 12   *Poems* by Emily Dickinson edited by Mabel Loomis Todd and Thomas Wentworth Higginson is published by Roberts Brothers of Boston.

1891 Nov. 9   *Poems* by Emily Dickinson, second series, edited by Thomas Wentworth Higginson and Mabel Loomis Todd is published by Robert Brothers of Boston.

1892 Jan. 1   **Ellis Island becomes chief immigration station of the United States.**

                 First gas-powered automobile developed in Springfield, Massachusetts, (25 miles from Amherst) by Frank and Charles Duryea. Driven down street in Springfield.

1894 Nov. 21   *Letters of Emily Dickinson*, 2 vols. Edited by Mabel Loomis Todd is published.

1895 Aug. 16   Austin dies.

1896 May 18   **Plessy v. Ferguson Supreme Court ruling makes segregation legal, paving way for Jim Crow laws in the South.**

      Sept. 1   *Poems by Emily Dickinson*, third series, edited by Mabel Loomis Todd is published by Roberts Brothers of Boston.

      Nov. 16   Vinnie files a lawsuit against the Todds.

1898 Apr.   Lawsuit against the Todds ruled in Vinnie's favor.

1899 Nov. 16   Vinnie dies, willing the Homestead to Martha Dickinson.

1911   Thomas Wentworth Higginson dies.

1913 May 12   Susan Gilbert Dickinson dies, willing The Evergreens to daughter Martha.

1915   Martha Dickinson, as the only surviving heir, sells the Homestead to Rev. Harvey Parke, rector of the Episcopal Church, because of financial difficulties in maintaining two large, mostly unoccupied, homes. She keeps The Evergreens, which she lives in most summers.

1932 Oct. 14   Mabel Loomis Todd dies.

1943   Martha Gilbert Dickinson Bianchi dies divorced and childless. The Evergreens and all copyrights and ownership of Dickinson materials in Martha's possession passes to her executor, Alfred Leete Hampson, who had coedited with her volumes of Dickinson's poetry.

1947		Alfred Hampson marries Mary Landis, who shares in his love of The Evergreens. Neither make any changes, keeping it the way Martha left it.
1950		Alfred Leete Hampson dies. Mary stays on at The Evergreens, as the last individual guardian.
1963		Dickinson Homestead designated a National Historical Site.
1965		Priscilla Parke sells the Homestead to Amherst College, which uses it for faculty housing.
1977		Dickinson homes and neighborhood are put on the National Register as the Dickinson Historic District.
1988		Mary Landis Hampson dies. Evergreens transfers to the Martha Dickinson Bianchi Trust.
1996		Amherst College stops using the Dickinson Homestead for faculty housing, hires a curator, and opens portions of it as a museum.
1998		Structural restoration enables portions of The Evergreens to be opened on a limited basis to the public. The wallpaper and furnishings are still the originals put there by Austin and Susan Dickinson.
2003	July 1	The Homestead and The Evergreens are once again joined in single ownership after an 88-year separation. Both houses are owned by Amherst College, which maintains them as a single museum dedicated to sharing the Dickinson family legacy with the public.
2004	Apr. 3	The Evergreens nursey, Gib's room, is opened for public tours. After Gib's death, so shortly before the poet's, the room had been essentially closed for over 120 years.

Chapter 1

INTRODUCTION

. . . for the true lovers of the prose or poetry of Emily Dickinson,
explanation of her is as impertinent as unnecessary.
—Martha Dickinson Bianchi
Introduction to *Complete Poems of Emily Dickinson*, 1924

Emily Dickinson stood about five feet four inches tall and was of slender to medium build. She had fine, wavy chestnut-red hair, brown eyes, very white, lightly freckled skin, a long neck, and full lips set in an oval-shaped face.[1] She stepped softly but quickly and deliberately upon the earth. Acquaintances describe her voice as equally soft and sometimes childlike, but when she was ready to talk, she talked nonstop. In fact, her talk was full of opinions about a variety of subjects and utilized an ongoing smart sense of wit. Her conversation was so full of force that it once exhausted a veteran officer of the Civil War who had come to visit her. The officer wrote his wife that evening that he could barely keep up with Emily as she spoke, and he was glad he didn't live near her so as to be affronted with the experience on a more frequent basis. When it came to use of language, Emily Dickinson was a force to be reckoned with. Relatives, on the other hand, described her voice as low and rich as she would read letters from her older brother aloud to the family or occasionally read them a poem she had written. She was full of compassion for the less fortunate around her, not so much for those in economic hard times to which she could not relate but most especially for those who suffered from illness or grief over the loss of a loved one, which were experiences she knew intimately. This was a soft spot she never seemed to get over, and since illness and death came much more often and unexpectedly in her time during the nineteenth century, death was an unsettling mystery that she puzzled over and pondered all of her life.

She was an excellent student who loved her teachers and learning; she read widely, teaching herself as much, if not more, at home as she learned in a formal classroom. She was the kind of studious person who kept a large dictionary by her side when she wrote and often pored over it, studying its entries, their origins, and their alternate definitions for new and unique ways to use them in her work. Her teachers praised her early compositions and asked her to read them aloud to the class. Some of this early writing, playful and mischievous, was published anonymously in student publications.

Dickinson played the piano well and won awards in contests for her bread baking. Her bread was so well made (during a time that valued this task almost as an artform) that her father insisted she be the primary family baker. She liked to sketch cartoons inside letters she wrote to friends, which portrayed a vibrant sense of humor about politics and the personalities of people she and her correspondents knew in common. She dried the dishes while the family housekeeper washed, but she didn't like to clean house at all and left that task to the housekeeper or to her younger sister Vinnie as much as possible when the family could not afford to hire help.

Dickinson was frugal with time and didn't like to waste it in small talk with people she barely knew neither for political status nor for financial gain. Her father's position in town made this necessary for her family on a daily basis on the first floor of her house, and at her brother's house next door, and in the streets and shops of Amherst. Over time, she avoided involving herself in such boring situations and public places increasingly, until she managed to live almost exclusively in the relaxed, intimate company of her family, her dog Carlo, and the workers around her home. She maintained friendships through written correspondence where she could carefully compose her thoughts. She cherished letters written to her in reply, rereading them over and over in the solitary freedom of her room, behind a door she locked from the inside.

Emily Dickinson didn't like formal religion and never allowed herself to join the church her family attended regularly, eventually stopping attending herself entirely. However, there was something about the elegant words of the Bible she had grown up hearing and the fervor of faith she witnessed in people close to her that didn't allow her to dismiss altogether the possibility of an afterlife, the existence of God, or that a spiritual dimension might exist.

She loved the precision and clear observations of science, especially the earth sciences of botany and geology, but also the wondrous study of astronomy. She laughed easily and regularly got her hands dirty kneeling down in the garden, and she performed small experiments of her own by raising exotic plants in her conservatory. Dickinson also loved the precision of language and the deep ideas of literature, especially the poetry of British poets Browning and Brontë, as well as Shakespeare. She was well informed, reading the newspaper daily and discussing with her family the popular novels of her day, such as those by Brontë, Dickens, and Hawthorne.

As an aunt and neighbor, Dickinson was a special friend to children. She could be counted on to conspire with them to steal a cookie from the kitchen, or to lower some gingerbread she had made down in a basket outside her second-floor window as part of joining in their games in a playful way. Her dog, Carlo, a Newfoundland-St. Bernard mix, was a steady companion and of special comfort to her during 16 years of her adult life. Dickinson did not marry, but she was not afraid to love, and she seems to have had many loves walk in and out of her life at various times. Dickinson might agree that too much attention has been paid to their identities over the years, when it is the giving and receiving of love itself that matters most.

Like many women of her day, she was a frequent gift giver, often sending baked goods or a flower from her garden or conservatory in her letters, but increasingly sending a poem as a gift instead, or a letter that seemed to be more of a poem or a gift in itself, rather than an attempt to convey a simple message of regard. As the years wore on and Dickinson's life settled into the routine of an unmarried adult living in her father's house, she deepened her commitment to writing. She wrote from a need to write and a joy in language, and she is now known to have spent many nights staying up late in her room thinking and composing, and sewing together chosen poems into booklets of her own design. Her family and many of her correspondents knew of her interest, but fewer than a dozen of her poems were printed in her lifetime and most of these anonymously.

Dickinson more openly admired her father than her mother, who was often ill, but she had traits of them both in her personality. She loved reading and rigorous thought like her father; but she also preferred staying out of the limelight like her mother, and she was often ill like her, though never bedridden for as long. As the middle child, Dickinson admired and joked with her outgoing older brother Austin who, as the boy in the family, had so much more opportunity than she would ever have, and she leaned on her loyal younger sister Lavinia for emotional support and stability. Ironically, her own ambition and depth of emotional grasp, however, would outdo both of her siblings in terms of the reach of her impact and influence upon the world.

Emily Dickinson was a driven woman—a woman driven to create art. When she was alone and could do what she wanted, or even while performing routine household tasks, Emily Dickinson wrote extraordinary poems and letters. It is for this reason that we care about her life and attempt to study it today. Because of her lifestyle of avoiding the public, the people of her small town of Amherst, Massachusetts, used to talk. They talked as people of small towns sometimes talk about someone who appears to be different in any way from the accepted norms of their kind. Without the woman there to defend herself in these situations or to change the tone or direction of their stories, and with the Dickinsons being such a prominent family in town that they were visible and already talked about in so many other ways, the stories about Emily Dickinson grew until they took on near mythic proportions that continue to this day. Today, reclusive people are still thought to be strange or odd or not quite right—but they are given their space and are pretty much left alone. Dickinson's space, living in a family that was so much otherwise a part of the community, came at a price that she was aware of but did nothing to change. Her family and their employees protected her wishes, and so the mythmaking and gossip continued.

When she died, her sister found the poems. There were so many poems in Emily's room that at first Lavinia did not know what to do with them. She knew her sister liked to read and think and write, and Lavinia had worked around her in the house so as to allow her sister to do this as often as possible. However, she did not know that Emily had managed to write so many poems over the years—nearly 1,800 in all. Those poems would later be published amid clouds of controversy that only expanded the stories already circulating about their reclusive creator.

Today we would suspect this controversy might be an intentional way of promoting interest in the poems, but this was only partially true. The controversies were genuine and arose from many complicated factors. However, the poems are of such quality and depth that they stand alone in spite of the mysterious trappings surrounding their publication. They have been cherished, studied, and written about by millions of readers around the world, while at the same time their author became an enigma.

Interest in the poet in the early twenty-first century is at an all-time high. In 2004, there were at least three full-length scholarly biographies of Emily Dickinson in print, numbering several hundred pages each. An internet search yielded over 200,000 hits, and a database search of the *Modern Language Association International Bibliography* yielded over 2,000 scholarly books and articles about the poet and her works. The difficult task of translating Dickinson's short but complex verses into different languages is still being conducted around the world. In the United States, children as young as preschool age are exposed to the poems through picture books, and the poems are discussed in English classes from elementary school through graduate school.

An author's society dedicated to the poet was founded in 1986, and by 2004 had hundreds of members around the world. The society hosts regular international conferences dedicated exclusively to the poet, which present the latest research by scholars.[2] Starting in 2002, an internet bookseller offered an online course in Dickinson's life and poems to its global audience, which filled up on an ongoing basis. In New York City, annual 24-hour marathon readings of the poet's works, which so frequently deal with the subject of grief and death, came into vogue as a response to the terrorist attacks of September 11, 2001. There have been Internet discussion groups dedicated to the poet, some running several years. Annual visitors to the Dickinson home in Amherst number in the thousands. As more information about the poet is uncovered through ongoing research, and as appreciation for the value of her poetry expands around the globe through translations, the need for meeting the needs of different kinds of audiences interested in Emily Dickinson's life and her work increases.

This biography is intended for the young adult student and the general reader who would like an overview of the current scholarship regarding the poet's life. Its major sources include Dickinson's own writing—poems and letters as primary material, both in manuscript form as well as published editions and the online *Dickinson Electronic Archive*. In researching this life story, the author also used published letters and accounts of the poet's family members and friends, and unpublished letters, papers, and artifacts available in the important Dickinson collections housed at the Emily Dickinson Museum, Harvard University, Brown University, Amherst College, and the Jones Library in Amherst.

In addition to primary material, the author made full use of these scholarly biographies: Alfred Habegger's 2002, *My Wars Are Laid Away in Books: The Life of Emily Dickinson* and Richard B. Sewall's 1974, *The Life of Emily Dickinson* in 2 volumes. Students and readers who would like a more detailed account of Dickinson's life are encouraged to seek out these important works. Literary criticism of the poems and letters has also been a useful tool in composing this general biography, especially whenever it illuminated facets of Dickinson's interests and writing practices. Correspondence and interviews with the curators of both Dickinson houses, librarians involved with Dickinson materials, and other Dickinson scholars have been used to clarify other issues as well.

Due to Greenwood's permissions and style policy for this educational
biography series, direct quotes from the poems and letters are severely limited and in-text source citations are not provided in order to improve
readability for students and general readers. As a scholar, the author ap-
preciates the difficulty this house policy may cause serious researchers, but
she must refer them to the bibliography or to the occasional brief note for
source information at the end of each chapter. As an active member of the
Dickinson scholarly community, the author is also available through the
publisher to answer questions from readers about sources for specific information. Following the current practice in Dickinson scholarship,
poems are referred to by their first lines (since most are untitled) rather
than by editorial numbers from various printed editions. The edition used
for most poems is *The Manuscript Books of Emily Dickinson*, 2 vols., edited
by Ralph W. Franklin, Harvard University Press, 1981.

Scholarship in the late twentieth and early twenty-first century has
worked to debunk the clouds and layers of mythology surrounding the poet
and attempt to find the real Emily Dickinson. Despite well-intentioned efforts and some valuable successes, this goal has not been, and will likely
not ever be, completely achieved. This book will show that this fact has
as much to do with the poet herself as it does with what others have done
with her story over time. Over and over again, the life story of this artist
tells us to look to her work to find out all we want to know about her, but
perhaps the best way to appreciate this is to first look at what we think we
do know about her life to see why this is so. As the poet herself once said,
"Biography first convinces us of the fleeing of the Biographied—"[3]

When Emily Dickinson first introduced herself in person to a longtime correspondent who came to meet her at her house in Amherst, she
placed two daylilies in his hand and said "These are my introduction."[4]
While this is a mysterious way to introduce oneself, it is clear that the
flowers did the trick. They made the meeting not only special but even
more memorable than it was already likely to be, given that the visitor
had been corresponding with her for eight years. The flowers associated
the woman physically standing in front of him with the flowers he now
held in his hand—both were soft, intricate, delicate, but perhaps more
importantly—natural, real, and fully alive.

NOTES

1. See funeral record no. 31 in 1886 book of funeral director Edwin Marsh (in
Longsworth, *World*, p. 112); Dickinson letter to Thomas W. Higginson, July,
1862 (in Dickinson, *Letters*, ed. by Johnson, 3 vol., # 268); lock of Dickinson's

hair in Special Collections at Amherst College; dress replica at the Homestead; Dickinson daguerreotype, Amherst College; Bianchi, *Face to Face*; Col. Higginson letter to Mary Higginson qtd. in Dickinson, *Letters*, ed. by Johnson, 3 vol., # 342a.

2. The Emily Dickinson International Society; Special Collections, Jones Library.

3. Dickinson letter to Thomas Wentworth Higginson, February, 1885. (Dickinson, *Letters*, Johnson, ed., 3 vols.

4. Thomas W. Higginson letter to Mary Higginson, qtd. in Dickinson, *Letters*, ed. by Johnson, 3 vol., # 342a.

Chapter 2

ANCESTRY, EARLY LIFE, AND FAMILY

Emily Dickinson's parents were Emily Norcross Dickinson (1804–1882) of Monson and Edward Dickinson (1803–1874) of Amherst. They both came from families that were influential in their respective towns, which are only a few miles apart from one another in western Massachusetts. The poet's ancestral heritage through her parents' marriage on May 6, 1828, sets a foundation not only for her home life but also for the life of the community into which she would be born.

EMILY NORCROSS DICKINSON

The history of the poet's maternal line is sketchier than the Dickinson one, owing in part, no doubt, to the lack of attention paid to women's histories and lack of public documents about them over so many years. Dickinson's maternal grandmother was Betsey Fay, a woman who was born in 1777, a year after the signing of the Declaration of Independence. She lived until 1829, the year before the poet was born, so Emily never knew her grandmother. In 1798, Betsey Fay married Joel Norcross and went on to bear nine children, the third of whom, Emily Norcross, would later be the poet's mother and share her name. Other sibling names that would repeat in the family line included Austin Norcross and Lavinia Norcross. Austin Norcross would die in his twenties in 1824. Emily Norcross, next in age, would honor his life five years later by naming her first son after him. Betsey's daughter Lavinia Norcross, the next girl after the poet's mother by approximately eight years, would go on to bear the cousins the poet loved most, Frances and Louisa (whom Emily would call "Fanny and

Loo"). Among Betsey's nine children, then, there was an Austin, an Emily, and a Lavinia. Though there were other children in between, these three shared the same birth order as the Dickinson siblings a generation later. It is also interesting to note that besides the names they bore in common, Emily Dickinson and her mother were both the eldest daughters in their respective households.

The poet's grandmother, Betsey Fay Norcross, was devoted to her husband and nine children. She suffered the loss of four of her children during her lifetime, including her first and second born, both sons, who died in their early adulthood. She was described in her obituary written by her minister as "humble and retiring in her disposition"[1] and as a woman whose talents and caring nature were most evident in relation to her family and the domestic sphere. In addition to her family, however, Betsey enjoyed the company of several friends, principally through her church's First Female Praying Circle, and she participated in charitable activities. The fact that her husband maintained several businesses around Monson, that her family was large, and that the family took in boarders, made her a person well known in the community for the efficiency of her work and her hospitality. The word retiring then takes on curious meanings, especially since it would reappear later on in descriptions of both Betsey's daughter and her famous granddaughter, as well.

Of Betsey's five children who survived, only two were daughters, Emily and Lavinia. This is significant because mothers and daughters took care of the entire household in those days, so the larger the house and family and the fewer the daughters, the more work that fell upon each one. The Norcross house in Monson was a converted tavern, large enough to accommodate their big family as well as boarders. In addition, events such as the deaths of not only Austin in 1824, but also five-year-old Nancy in the same year, must have taken their toll on Emily Norcross, who was still just a teenager herself. By all accounts, Emily Norcross worked hard as a girl and young woman, a fact that is often omitted in consideration of her later life as the poet's sickly, retiring mother.

Joel Norcross, Emily Dickinson's maternal grandfather, was a successful businessman in Monson and owned the most valuable property in town. He was a chief stockholder of the Hampden Cotton Manufacturing Company and had his own farm. His brother and other relatives owned other businesses in town, such as stores and taverns. Joel was wealthy by small-town standards and was therefore well known but not always well liked around Monson.

Joel Norcross did give of his time and treasure to the community, including helping to organize the Union Charitable Society of Monson's

First Congregational Church and building a branch chapel of the church in the nearby town of Maine, Massachusetts. His most substantial philanthropic donations, however, were for his favorite cause, Monson Academy. The academy was incorporated in 1804 and continued to be regarded as one of the best western Massachusetts schools until the 1830s. Joel was its largest individual benefactor.

Born in 1804, Emily Norcross was Betsey and Joel's third child; she would become the eldest surviving child after the deaths of her two older brothers. In many ways, her growing-up experience mirrored her famous namesake's years later. Her family had extended family in town, was well known, and she lived in a house that entertained visitors regularly. With her sister Lavinia, she cared for her mother Betsey when she grew ill. This was particularly the case when Betsey confronted the deaths of four of her nine children.

Bedridden women fighting illness in the nineteenth century could have been fighting diseases and ailments that are regularly treated with medications today. Severe diseases such as consumption (or tuberculosis) were common and devastating in the period. There was little medical help available for such common ailments as hypertension, heart disease, diabetes, gynecological infections, postpartum and other depressions, physical changes of life such as menopause, and others. The prevalence of multiple pregnancies during a period when prenatal and postnatal care was also not as sophisticated as it is now wore on women's bodies. Often the only defense they had in the form of home treatment was to take the advice of male doctors and their nurses—usually their own mothers, daughters, and sisters—and take to their beds to get as much rest as possible.

Added to this medical defenselessness was a patriarchal society that believed that women should be kept indoors, at home, and protected, and a legal system that limited women's rights and opportunities. It is small wonder that women who suffered with various ailments over their lifetimes were often described as invalids, sickly, hysterical, or chronically ill. No one today would expect a woman with chronic hypertension to suffer through the deaths of one or more of her children and not be hit with a physical setback, probably with a bout of depression to go with it; and this was the type of scenario women of the period lived out over and over again. The period of the nineteenth century is filled with accounts of women caring for their bedridden counterparts within their families, and the Norcross-Dickinson story is no different.

With her father's wealth and support of education, Emily Norcross had the opportunity to be educated at Monson Academy, and then later at the

Herrick School in New Haven, Connecticut, where her brother attended Yale. She was intelligent, interested in books and religion, and held high standards of moral conviction. When Edward Dickinson came to Monson in January of 1826 on business, she found an instant rapport with him; however, her letters to him during their epistolary courtship were sparsely written and few between. The poet's later accusation that her mother did not care for thought may have come from her mother's hard years of labor as a young woman helping to run a large household while helping her mother go through the deaths of four of her children. Early hard, physical labor, especially under dire circumstances, tends to keep one's priorities set on practical matters and often does not afford one the luxury of time spent in the deep thought that Emily Dickinson grew up enjoying. On the other hand, the poet was not foreign to physical work herself, especially at certain periods when the family was unable to hire help, and perhaps she erroneously measured the depth of her mother's thoughts in proportion to the rarity of her sharing them. Both women enjoyed their solitude.

In 1828 when Emily Norcross left home to move with her new husband into a duplex in Amherst they shared with the Montague family, she put her intelligence and high standards into the practical matter of managing a spotless, efficient kind of household that would be comfortable for the type of guests she, and especially her husband, expected to cultivate. She knew that Edward, like her father, Joel, was ambitious and had influential family connections in the community, and she no doubt shared in his vision of establishing a new branch of both families that would continue to contribute in a prominent way. Emily Norcross Dickinson learned early that daughters care for their ill mothers, and some might say that she prepaid dues owed to her daughters in her relationship with their grandmother, which left her with less physical and emotional energy for her own children. Betsey Fay Norcross bore children and worked hard until she was spent and needed help; Emily and Lavinia Norcross provided it. In turn, Emily Norcross Dickinson expected, and received, the same amount of doting devotion from the poet and her sister.

In her letters, the poet suggests that her relationship with her mother was not an intellectual one, but a mother omitted from one's letters and artistic and other interests is not a mother absent in life. Dickinson's early health and upbringing were certainly tended to and accomplished by her mother. Mrs. Dickinson took the job of parenthood seriously, if perhaps a bit dutifully, by reading up on the practice of childrearing early in her marriage and even taking notes from sermons as a single woman about what mothers should teach their children concerning morality. The functioning of the family's responsibilities for Edward's public events needed to run smoothly and without a hitch. No doubt she read faithfully her copy of *The Frugal Housewife* by Lydia Maria Child, which Edward gave her in about 1830. Consulting this book and others for advice on house-keeping and child rearing shows more of a literary tendency than has been previously afforded the poet's mother. Edward and Emily N. Dickinson's high standards required knowledge and discipline, especially since many functions often involved opening their home and hosting visiting officials and other guests there.

Traits the poet appeared to share with her mother include her appreci-ation of home and nature. As a young woman, Emily Norcross missed Monson while she was away at Herrick, and she enjoyed and appreciated country life, commenting easily on the pleasant songs of birds. If she did not enjoy writing, she did read faithfully and apparently could turn a witty phrase in conversation.

That the poet said in a letter that she did not hold much affection for her mother until their roles reversed in later years and she was tending more to her mother's needs, suggests that there may have been an ongo-ing battle of wills between them in the household, perhaps over how best to spend one's time.

Some scholars argue that Dickinson suffered from an emotionally dis-tant mother and grew up missing that affection all of her life. They point to her frequent praise and admiration for her father in her letters. In part, children learn to honor a parent by modeling the respect the other parent pays to him or her, and this was likely a factor in Dickin-son's feelings for her busy and accomplished father. Her mother and the entire household clearly revolved around his comings and goings, and much of the town did as well. That perhaps the poet did not learn to ap-preciate her mother's contribution may be as much a testament to Ed-ward's self-centeredness and neglect of teaching his children to respect their mother's importance in their lives as it was a factor of the times in which she lived. Like many men of the period, Edward downplayed women's roles.

Rather than lack of affection per se, it may be the case that the Emilies, both mother and daughter, were very much alike and perhaps did not get along especially well because of it—a condition that has been known to happen in many families. There are several letters where the poet does not sign "Emily" but chooses other names or spellings, such as "Emilie," perhaps to distinguish herself from her mother. Perhaps there was some subconscious competition for Edward's attention, or perhaps Emily the elder was as strong-willed that bread be baked a certain way and silver be polished to a specific sheen as Emily the younger was fierce about guarding time in the day for reflection and engaging in verbal fencing matches. Given the difference in their upbringing, one with more emphasis on and need for the practical, the other with the liberty to pursue a few more of her own interests because of her comparatively comfortable life, differences over how best to spend one's time may be as good a reason as any for tensions that may have existed between them.

Whatever their reasons, the poet gradually withdrew from the public and attention outside the Homestead, and her mother may have gradually withdrawn from the family as well, having suffered an overdose of family responsibilities too early in life to fully enjoy her spirited and independent children. Whatever the cause, in both cases in later years the solution to dealing with circumstances the Emilies would rather not contend with apparently fell into a mutual pattern of turning inward, spending more time in their respective chambers, and closing the door.

EDWARD DICKINSON

What scholars know about the poet's paternal side of the family, which is considerably more than is known about the maternal side, despite more recent efforts at remedying that problem,[2] stretches back as far as seventeenth-century England. Puritans Nathaniel and Ann Gull Dickinson left Billingborough parish in Lincolnshire around 1637 for America, arriving in Wetherfield, Connecticut, which was then not much more than a British outpost. They came, as did many of the Puritans, for religious freedom. In 1659, the couple and their children moved into Native American Norwottuck territory in what is now western Massachusetts. They and others established a town they called Hadley, which still exists today. In Hadley, Nathaniel began what would be a Dickinson family tradition—he became heavily involved in the establishment of the town's government, education, and religious infrastructures. During fighting with the Indians in 1675, Nathaniel and Ann lost three of their nine sons. Despite this diminishment, the family extended its line in depth and breadth in the community and the surrounding rural area.

In 1759, a new town was formed out of the eastern end of Hadley. It was named Amherst after Lord Jeffrey Amherst, among whose claims to fame included an alarming desire and strategy for genocide against the Native Americans—he suggested that they be eradicated by having blankets infected with smallpox thrown over them. As a large family from Hadley, the Dickinsons populated Amherst as it developed.

The poet's grandfather, Samuel Fowler Dickinson (1775–1838), grew up in Amherst and attended Dartmouth where he graduated with a degree in Latin, thinking he might become a minister. Like his male predecessors before him, Samuel was a leader in the community, but perhaps unlike some of them, he did not always have the stability of character to handle the responsibilities that went with this distinction. Rejecting the ministry but still clinging to the doctrine of Calvinism, Samuel became tutored in law by Judge Simeon Strong in Amherst. Soon Samuel owned wide land holdings in the area that earned him the honorary designation of Squire. While the land in his name bestowed him power in the community, behind the scenes, Squire Dickinson was not quite making all of the payments on the mortgages. His prestige grew as he cofounded Amherst College, but at the same time, his own personal and business affairs undermined the financial stability this should have brought to his family.

Samuel married Lucretia Gunn of Montague on March 21, 1802, who was by most accounts, reserved in nature and abrupt in her dealings with others. Many years later, her grandchildren, the poet and her siblings, remarked at their own occasional losses of temper or foul moods claiming that it was not their own personalities but their Grandmother Gunn's that was manifesting itself. Her daughter, Elizabeth, born after Edward, inherited some of her mother's traits—Emily trembled at the sound of her boots. The poet once called her the only male relative in the family on the female side.

By 1813, Samuel and Lucretia had a large family with five children; four more would eventually arrive. They needed a larger home. The Squire built the first brick house in Amherst on an elevation above Main Street. It was built in the Federal style, with four large rooms on both the first and second floors. Several additions and alterations later, this structure became the Dickinson Homestead where the poet was born and where she eventually died, though she lived at one other location for a time in between. Squire Dickinson, seeking to establish a legacy in the town, had no idea how important this brick house would become to American letters.

Edward Dickinson (1803–1874), the poet's father, was the eldest of his parents' nine children and lived, perhaps, most aware of the continuing pressures of his father's unsupported ambition. One example of this was that in his sophomore year at Yale, Edward had to drop out two different times and go home to take classes at Amherst College because his father could not afford Yale's tuition. He eventually did graduate, but with a 2.4 average, not with the high honors one might expect of the future father of a genius.

Interestingly, the young Edward Dickinson took a special interest in women's conditions in society at his time. Instead of recognizing their plight in terms of women's suffrage and fighting for increased women's rights, as would increase in popularity a few decades later, Edward took the opposing view that women should be protected from the messy and cruel world that existed outside the domestic sphere. He interpreted his role as helping them deal with the roughness and unfairness of society by keeping the women he loved financially secure (something his own father had not accomplished) and at home in a comfortable house that he provided.

Influenced by a book *Coelebs in Search of a Wife* by Hannah More, (*Coelebs* is Latin for bachelor), in 1827, Edward helped found the first newspaper in Amherst, *The New-England Inquirer*. In it he wrote five articles about the education of females. Using an anonymous penname, Coelebs, Edward described the role of women's education as enhancing their ability to perform at domestic tasks and to be a social partner to their husbands' professional lives in that they may hold up their end of intelligent conversations without dominating them. In no way, Coelebs asserted, should women ever overtake men in such conversations or in literary matters, such as reading and writing novels. Rather, they remain happier if they sacrifice their energies in these regards to the maintenance of a warm and orderly household.

While Edward's writing was harsh enough to receive criticism even in its own day, his beliefs on the subject are actually more complex than his young bachelor writings would suggest. He later bought books, for example, for his daughter Emily, then asked her not to read them. He outwardly put down women having a role in public literary life, yet at the same time he read their books. This ambivalence suggests that Edward had perhaps the secret desire to see women be intelligent, educated, and their writing be published, but he also held a fear of what might happen to the sanctity of the family afterward if this were to happen. Ambition had ruined his family's stability once with his father. What could happen if women were allowed to act on their ambitions at will as well? Edward's urge to protect his family overrode all else. Small wonder that many years later, his daughter the genius poet would find herself negotiating publication between the private and public spheres.

Added to school troubles brought on by his father's overreaching ambition, Edward knew that his father was putting up the Homestead as collateral to pay for debt after debt. This meant that rather than a fixed place of valuable property from which the family could draw security and prosper, Samuel had so many liens against it that the family really didn't own the Homestead at all. Not only that, but Edward's father had borrowed money from almost every relative with means, degrading any safety net they would have for the future and putting more and more family members at financial risk and strain.

While Edward's younger brother William bucked at the foolishness of their father and sought work elsewhere, Edward, as the eldest and with his views of the males in the family as protectors, shouldered more of the responsibility of rebuilding the family name. Whether through a sense of duty or of personal pride, Edward apparently made a decision that he would work to bring back the family from the brink of financial ruin and disgrace.

In the meantime, the serious young man met Emily Norcross when he sat next to her at a chemistry lecture in Monson. In courtly fashion, on February 8, 1826, Edward entered into a wooing correspondence with the woman who would be the poet's mother. He told her of his affections, and she replied in kind, though her letters were never as forthcoming as his and were characteristically and sometimes frustratingly for Edward, short and far between. They courted for two years in this way; Edward sent Emily Norcross 70 letters; she sent him only 24.

In Vivian Pollak's edition of the courtship letters, A Poet's Parents, readers glimpse a view of Edward's personality and treatment of women. Small wonder his eldest daughter grew up to prefer staying at home when her father wrote the excerpt below in a letter to her mother several years earlier when they were engaged. The letter appears on page 174 of the collection:

I can't say that I approve of your being "out almost every evening"—
I am in constant anxiety that you will expose yourself so much that
you will destroy your health. You *must be a little more careful*, Emily—
I can not feel easy to think, every evening, whether it "rains or
shines" that you are *out*, whether I know it, or not.

On page 193 of the collection, Emily Norcross responds to another of Edward's letters, closing her short note with her characteristic, quick style that so frustrated the young lawyer—"I now leave you yet my thoughts will not cease to act. This haste you must excuse." To win her hand, Edward had to not only win over Emily Norcross but also her father, Joel, whose standing in Monson made him a particularly good prize to have on Edward's side. In addition, Edward needed to establish himself more fully in his law practice. Showing some of his father's ambition, the poet's father managed to succeed at all of these.

EARLY FAMILY LIFE

On May 6, 1828, the coupled married and moved into one-half of a house in Amherst that Edward had repaired and furnished for their married life and that his bride-to-be's father had previously visited and approved. Joel Norcross even sent a new cast-iron stove as a gift to be installed before the wedding. The other half of the house was occupied by Jemima Montague, so the young Dickinsons began their lives together in shared housing. Edward's father owned the house, at least on paper, so Edward believed this benefit would give them a foothold and a start.

Unfortunately, a month after their marriage, Samuel Dickinson was discovered to be, for all intents and purposes, bankrupt. He had not paid the taxes on several of his properties, which put the Montague house at risk. Keeping his head and developing still more of the set jaw and stoic attitude that people in town would come to know so well, Edward consulted with his father-in-law, Joel Norcross, who had been successful in Monson without the backsliding his own father had experienced. Through that advice and with some help from his cousin Nathan Dickinson, Edward managed to secure, for the time being, his right to the property that he had repaired and refurnished. In the meantime, Emily Norcross Dickinson became pregnant.

The Norcrosses responded to Emily's predicament with support and concern. Her sister Lavinia spoke for mother Betsey and others in the family when she wrote that they wished Emily would not take it upon herself to work so hard at scrupulous housekeeping with no help. When they sent her a recommended woman to hire, Emily did not keep the person employed. Preferring to do all the work herself and without the medical care hard workers like her benefit from today, Emily's health began to suffer. The many years of running her mother's household, and now her own when she was newly married, pregnant, and under financial strain in shared housing, began taking their toll. After at least two failures at sending her someone to help her, the Norcrosses finally sent their own housekeeper, Mary, to lend her a hand. That the poet's mother's ambition and pride matched her father's is evident in the fact that she took in boarders from Amherst College during the very semester when she would deliver her first child. At a time when the young couple was trying to make a go of it, Mrs. Dickinson was as hard a worker as her husband. Like him in Amherst, she had come from a family prominent in Monson and did not want to lose face in the community over money.

The boarders did not work out much longer after William Austin Dickinson was born on April 16, 1829. Despite the joy of bearing their first child, the couple continued to endure further hard times early in their marriage with the death of Emily's mother, Betsey Fay Norcross, on September 5, 1829, and the news from now-married Nathan Dickinson in Michigan that he could no longer help Edward financially with the Montague house. Edward again sought his father-in-law's advice (not his money and not his own father's help), but this time he managed to work out a deal before Joel Norcross's reply arrived.

In March 1830, Edward Dickinson bought one-half of the Homestead back from his cousin Nathan. They would be moving from one duplex situation to another, but Edward believed the Homestead, his childhood home, would eventually offer his little family the security they so badly needed. Again that summer, with a toddler underfoot and now pregnant once more, Emily took in boarders to help with the finances. By September 1, the Dickinsons moved to the Homestead on Main Street, occupying the west half of the house, with Edward's parents and remaining siblings living on the east side. It is a testament to Squire Dickinson's (Samuel Fowler) instability that he was not able to offer this part of the house to his young son and his family himself because he did not own it.

That fall, news came from Monson that Joel Norcross would soon be remarrying. This was an essential move since Betsey's death and Mrs. Dickinson's marriage had left only Lavinia to care for the tavern house and her siblings, Alfred and Joel Warren. Sarah Vaill, the poet's step-grandmother, had been a teacher. She was well thought of, in her forties, and had never previously married. She had a good disposition. She and Joel married January 6, 1831, and she became the only grandmother the poet knew on her mother's side.

By the time the baby girl was born who would, years later, grow to be of such interest around the world, a small sense of security about their living arrangements appears to have been achieved by the young family living in the Homestead. Edward held the mortgage in his name for the west side of the house. It seemed that as long as they could make the payments, they would not have to contend with the property being sold out from under them again, at least for awhile. Perhaps their new surroundings added to the pleasure of the birth of their first baby girl. Edward recorded their first daughter's birth in his wife's Bible: "Emily Elisabeth, their second child / was born Dec. 10. 1830. at 5. o'clock A.M."[3] The poet was born in the Homestead, in the same side of the house where her famous bedroom would be visited by thousands of poetry pilgrims years later. Given how important the house became to her life and work, it seems now that there is no other place on earth where the poet could have possibly been born.

With the addition of a second daughter, this one named after their mother's dear sister, Lavinia, on February 28, 1833, the poet's immediate family was complete. Her younger sister was called Vinnie in order to distinguish her from Aunt Lavinia. Unfortunately, after Vinnie's birth, the family's financial troubles resurfaced. Edward's law business suffered from fewer litigations around town as a result of recent church revivals, and he began to think about leaving Amherst altogether, getting a new start elsewhere out from under the shadow of his father's law practice and poor financial reputation. He was forced to sell back his portion of the house to his cousin and his partner, who in turn, sold the whole building to General David Mack, Jr., a wealthy man from the west. As it turned out, it was Squire Dickinson who left the Homestead and Amherst and moved west, not Edward, and the poet never saw her grandfather again after she was three years old. When the Macks arrived, they were content to let out half of the house, yet again, as a duplex. However, they wanted the west half not the east, so the Dickinsons had to pick up their belongings and move across the hall to the other side of the house. They lived this way, sharing the small living space beside the Mack family, who began adding onto their side of the house making it larger and more comfortable, until the poet was nine years old.

During the years in the small eastern half of the Homestead, with the Squire now gone, Edward managed to build up his law practice. He began to step out from under his father's shadow, gaining the reputation of a responsible man of character who kept his promises and paid his debts. His income also increased when he was selected as Amherst College treasurer. Though he was the son of the cofounder of the college, Edward must have taken personal pride in the appointment, due to his father's very public mishandling of his own finances.

CHILDHOOD

Sometime around the first of April, 1840, the poet and her family moved to a house on West Street (now Pleasant Street), a large frame structure that Edward purchased for $3,000. For the first time, through her parents' hard efforts, the family had a whole house and over two acres of land entirely to themselves. These years marked some of the poet's happiest and would also plant a few of the seeds of what grew later to become some of her most intense preoccupations.

Among the Dickinsons' three children, Austin (the family called him by his middle name), the oldest and a boy, was the one who was expected to do well in school and make a name for himself in the world. Only 15 months younger, Emily as the middle child grew up very close to Austin as a play-mate and no doubt shared some of the run-off in terms of educational experiences inside the home. Their mother took child rearing as seriously as she did her housework, reading books that covered both subjects to learn as much as she could. As an educated woman from a family that valued learning, Mrs. Dickinson surely saw to it that Austin, Emily, and later Vinnie had books and paper and were schooled in the Bible. Edward recommended reading for his children in terms of children's periodicals of the day to which he subscribed and notified his wife that he expected them to use.

Several of Emily's poems and letters refer to when she or the poem's speaker was a "boy." It is difficult to imagine the first two siblings so close in age not enjoying similar experiences early in life. When Austin was taught the alphabet, for example, it seems natural that Emily would have been sitting there right alongside him. Perhaps Emily recalled these early days when she felt she was on an equal footing with Austin for all the possibilities in the world. Perhaps their playtimes early on at the Homestead and then later at West Street, running through the fields, would have been similar up to a certain age. If Austin was trained at home with the high expectation for a life in the public eye of business and the community, Emily soon learned that her parents had different expectations for her and her sister. As the boy, Austin was assigned the typical outdoor chores that would help the family, such as fetching water from the barn well (the Macks had control of the house well), while the girls' domestic duties were almost all indoors.

What was Emily Dickinson like as a child? There are not many surviving records to go by for clues, but there are a few glimpses provided by the letters of relatives. Aunt Lavinia Norcross, for example, gives the earliest known written account of the poet speaking. With Emily's mother pregnant again and ill, the move from the west side of the Homestead to the east about to transpire, and little Austin and Emily under her feet, the family arranged for two-and-a-half-year-old Emily (perhaps busy by comparison to Austin, who would have made it out of his "terrible twos" by then) to visit the Norcrosses for awhile to help ease the strain. Aunt Lavinia called her niece "Elizabeth" to avoid confusing her with her mother. On a carriage ride taking her from Amherst to Monson for an extended stay, Aunt Lavinia decided to try to outrun an approaching storm. When the lightning struck and the thunder rolled, and the rain came down in the woods outside of Belchertown, Lavinia was gratified that their horse did not seem to mind but kept right on galloping along. She reported to her sister later that "Elizabeth" called the lightning "the fire" and asked to be taken to her mother right away.[4]

In contrast to the strains on her immediate family that probably made the two-year-old Emily particularly difficult to handle at the time, at the Norcross's, Emily amused her grandfather Joel with her "sports," and behaved well for her age in church. When she spoke loudly in the pew, Grandfather Joel gave her a "pat," that Aunt Lavinia conveyed got her attention but did not hurt her. Young Emily probably saw a piano for the first time at the Norcross's; she called it "the moosic."[5] While Aunt Lavinia, who was then only 21, was still adjusting to congenial Sarah as her new stepmother, she became attached to little Emily immediately, writing to her sister during the duration of the visit that Elizabeth ate and slept well, was affectionate and endearing to those who cared for her, and was quite content in the Norcross household. She would talk about her parents and "little Austin"[6] on occasion but was apparently comfortable enough that she did not ask to go home. Given her mother's propensity for seriousness and reserve, not to mention the fact that she didn't feel well much of the time and had an unsettled household arrangement, it would seem that Aunt Lavinia provided, perhaps, a welcome sense of calm security and outward affection for the little girl. Perhaps young Aunt Lavinia (eight years younger than the poet's mother) was the parent the poet would later wish she'd had when she claimed that she'd had no mother. However, if this had been so, perhaps the little girl would not have grown to be the woman who compressed so many of her strong feelings into exquisite lines of poetry.

SAMPLER

Dickinson returned to her family after a month at the Norcross's, and though she was often sickly, she grew and prospered, particularly once the family had settled in at the West Street house. The house was embraced by rose bushes, and orchards of fruit trees gave blooms and fragrance to the property as well as fresh produce, jams, and jellies to the Dickinson table. When she was not outside playing with Austin, Emily learned to sew and do needlework, among other household chores. Her cross-stitched sampler, now kept in the Emily Dickinson Room at Harvard, shows either a lack of skill or care or both in this domestic art. While the design and verse is more elaborate than her cousin, Emily Lavinia Norcross's[7] (Hiram and Amanda Brown Norcross's daughter) which may have been sewn at approximately the same time, the poet's stitches are not counted out properly so that the popular verse has to be squeezed in above the ends of four of its six lines. This is carefully done, however, so that the entire verse is present and readable: "Jesus Permit Thy Gracious Name to (stand) / As the first efforts of an infant's hand / And while her fingers oer this canvas (move) / Engage her tender heart to seek thy (love) / With thy dear children let her share a Part / And write thy name thyself upon her (heart)."[8] Interestingly, the attention to spacing of words across a line would later fascinate Dickinson scholars engaged in study of the poet's manuscripts.

The design of the 20-inch-square sampler includes the verse centered underneath alphabets of upper- and lowercase letters, as was customary. The cross-stitch stitches are sewn on linen, probably in silk thread. Though some of her stitches vary from this technique, Dickinson sewed most of the cross-stitches bottom left to top right then covered that stitch bottom right to top left. Below the verse is a house stitched prominently (and, for Dickinson, prophetically) in the center. The house has two chimneys and a large door and five windows across the front with two more windows sewn along the side. There are two trees stitched on either side of the house; portions of these are done in long-stitch embroidery rather than cross-stitch. An urn of flowers sits on the ground at the left side of the house, and a fence runs along the ground on the other side. The entire design is finished off with a border characteristic of samplers, though again, the pattern Dickinson used was more elaborate than her cousin's.

Perhaps disapproving of its imperfection as a form of domestic art, the young poet neither signed nor dated her sampler, as was the usual custom. It is another of the many absences that would characterize both her life and the record of it. Perhaps, again prophetically, she objected to signing her name to the verse, which asked that Jesus sign his name on her heart. It is likely that already as a young girl, as later, she did not want to attach her name to that which she did not believe. It may be, as Ethel Stanwood Bolton suggests about creative girls in general in *American Sampler,* that Dickinson purposely sewed her sampler poorly or did not complete it as an act of rebellion against this enforced ritual of female domesticity:

As one contemplates the millions of stitches worked by these young girls, one wonders what their thoughts were as they sewed them. Children are conventional and conservative beings, and so, perhaps the universality of the employment kept most from boredom. But there must always have been a residuum of the discouraged, and of the rebels "who hated every stitch," and so made their samplers badly or left them unfinished if they could possibly shirk their task. A plodding schoolmistress, whose whole artistic horizon was bored by alphabets and numerals, must have been torture to an imaginative child, who saw all nature to mimic with her colored threads. [9]

That Dickinson may have purposely sewn her sampler poorly or did not complete it as an act of rebellion against this enforced ritual of female domesticity seems, at the very least, plausible. One is reminded of the poem about unfinished sewing, dated by editor Ralph W. Franklin as approximately 1863, written during her peak years of poetic production:

> Dont put up my Thread & Needle -
> I'll begin to Sow -
> When the Birds begin to whistle -
> Better stitches - so -
>
> These were bent - my sight got crooked -
> When my mind - is plain
> I'll do seams - a Queen's endeavor
> Would not blush to own -
>
> Hems - too fine for Lady's tracing
> To the sightless knot -
> Tucks - of dainty interspersion -
> Like a dotted Dot -
>
> Leave my Needle in the furrow -
> Where I put it down -
> I can make the zigzag stitches
> Straight - when I am strong -
>
> Till then - dreaming I am sowing
> Fetch the seam I missed -
> Closer - so I - at my sleeping -
> Still surmise I stitch -[10]

While the poem is ostensibly about getting too tired in the evening to sew straight and leaving the rest of the work until the morning, "When the Birds begin to whistle -," the line "When my mind is plain" suggests that the speaker's mind is not plain when the sewing goes badly, but that the mind is occupied, filled with ideas that make the hand shake and the attention wander. This unplain mind is a mind that would rather dream (create art) than sew. However, the speaker asks her addressee to not put up her needle and thread for her but to "Leave my Needle in the furrow - " and "Fetch the seam

I missed - / Closer" so that she can still think she is sewing while she is dreaming. The pun on sew with "sow" and "furrow" equates the domestic work of sewing with the other necessary work of farming, planting small seeds or stitches that must be straight and planted where one is "strong." So, while at the same time the poem expresses the desire to dream (create) rather than sew, there is an apologetic tone to the poem that conveys a sense of duty recognized and the will to return to it once dreaming has ended and the mind is "plain" again. In fact, there is a promise to sew even better in the morning— seams a Queen would be proud to own; hems too fine to trace; sightless knots; and dainty tucks. In short, the poem is a promise—don't take away my thread and needle, the speaker seems to be saying. I will come back stronger, with clearer vision and sew even better after I am done dreaming/creating with my mind that is right now otherwise occupied.

This struggle between domestic duty and artistic endeavor is a recurrent motif in Dickinson's poetry. Her unfinished sampler sewn as a young girl is, perhaps, an example of physical artifact as precursor of this later theme in her work.

* * *

One of the features that would stay with the poet from her childhood at the West Street house was the presence of the town cemetery right behind it. Numerous funeral processions passed by the house, and Dickinson, who was often kept home from school for illness or bad weather, could easily and clearly see the carriages and mourners dressed in black. With frequent deaths in the nineteenth century from tuberculosis and other diseases they were defenseless against, deaths were a more frequent, everyday experience. Many scholars have attributed Dickinson's fascination with death to this early familiarity with its ceremony.

Not only that, but Dickinson heard about deaths of people she knew and probably attended several funerals. Over the span of a only a few months in early 1844, when the poet was just 13, a particularly large number of deaths affected notable people and families whom she or her parents knew in the town. The series ended with the death of someone quite close to Emily. The first was the death of Deborah Fiske, the wife of an Amherst College professor. Dickinson probably attended her funeral. Harriet W. Fowler, the wife of another professor and the daughter of Amherst native Noah Webster, followed her. Dickinson knew the children of these women. Lastly, and the most traumatic for Emily, was the death of her friend and cousin, Sophia Holland.

The young poet was allowed to watch over Sophia's sick bed in an attempt to comfort both girls. Sophia was ill with "brain fever." When Sophia became delirious, Emily was sent out of the room on doctor's orders. She begged to return for one last look. When the doctor finally relented and allowed her back in, the future poet removed her shoes and tiptoed into the room. What she saw was to traumatize her and change her life forever.

At only 13, when she gazed on the face of her beloved friend who was very near death, she could not escape the way the girl's face looked healthier than it had in days. The most mysterious aspect to her was an unearthly smile that lit up Sophia's features. Mesmerized by the mystery of that smile, Dickinson allowed herself to be led away by friends moments before the girl died. Years later, she revealed how much that experience had haunted her, sending her into a deep depression (called melancholy) that required a month's stay in Boston, again with Aunt Lavinia, to help break it.

Death surrounded her all the time. These episodes came so close together and ended with such a traumatic experience for her at such a young age. These facts, along with the existence of the cemetery behind her West Street house, may help readers understand Dickinson's apparent preoccupation with death in her poems.

However much she may have prospered in the roomy house at West Street, there would be one last move for the family to find secure housing. That move would be a final one for the poet as well, and one that would impact her life and American literature in profound, yet then unknown, ways.

NOTES

1. Qtd. in Habegger, "Wars," p. 27.
2. See Ackmann, "Matrilineage"; Bernhard, "Portrait."
3. Qtd. in Habegger, "Wars," p. 71.
4. Qtd. in Sewall, Life, p. 323.
5. Qtd. in Sewall, Life, p. 324.
6. Qtd. in Sewall, Life, p. 324.
7. See Longsworth, World, p. 24.
8. Dickinson sampler, Emily Dickinson Room, Harvard University.
9. Bolton, American Sampler, p. 397.
10. Dickinson, The Manuscript Books of Emily Dickinson, 2 vol. edited by Ralph W. Franklin.

Chapter 3

EDUCATION, RELIGION, AND
EARLY FRIENDSHIPS

Amherst, Massachusetts, in the nineteenth century was a small agricultural and college town where everyone was acquainted, and organized religion played an integral part in citizens' everyday lives. Emily Dickinson was a member of one of the town's most prominent families with many relatives living nearby. Both as a woman and a poet, she was influenced heavily not only by her formal education and her experience with formal religion but also by close friendships and the general atmosphere in the town in which her family played such an integral leadership role.

Dickinson's first formal school experience is generally agreed on by scholars to be at the West Center District School at what would later be 220 North Pleasant Street in Amherst. Rather than a private school, the poet probably attended this public school because of her father's election to Amherst's General School Committee in 1832, which signified his commitment to public education. Like other children of the time, Emily was often kept home from school if the weather were inclement or if she felt in the slightest bit ill. Fear of consumption and other diseases they had no medicines to cure propelled parents toward this reluctance to take any risks with their children in terms of health. Girls, with their presumed frailty in body and lower educational expectations, were particularly vulnerable to this precaution.

The poet probably entered West Center in the fall of 1835, when she was not quite five years old. There, she would have most likely learned her lessons in the alphabet and reading through drills with *The New England Primer*, and other schoolbooks of the time. She stayed at home on bad weather days, when Austin went to school alone. Later on, when their youngest sibling, Lavinia, went to school, their father would tell her to look out for her sister, Emily. Somehow, early on, the poet earned a family reputation for being either more susceptible to illness from the elements, or having particularly bad cases of illnesses when she did get them, or both. In any event, of the three Dickinson children, Emily was the one the other two looked after from quite early on. This habit continued into adulthood.

When she was not at school, it is also likely that her mother continued her lessons at home. Edward purchased subscriptions to children's publications such as *Parley's Magazine* and the *Sabbath School Visiter* for his children. While her mother had more education than many women because of Joel and Betsey Norcross's commitments to education, writing had never apparently been the poet's mother's strong suit. It is questioned whether the girl's frequent absences from early schooling and her mother's imperfect writing skills may have contributed to some of the peculiarities of the poet's later spelling and grammatical idiosyncrasies.

AMHERST ACADEMY

In the fall of 1840, when she was nine years old, Emily Dickinson was one of the first girls to attend the previously all-male Amherst Academy. She attended school there for seven years, though, again, these years were spotty in terms of attendance. For its time, Amherst Academy had a particularly rigorous curriculum that served the poet in good stead later on. She took classes in subjects such as English (including literature, composition, and speaking skills), Latin, geology, algebra, geometry, botany, history, "mental philosophy," (a precursor to today's psychology) and church history. She and her classmates wrote a composition every other week, which they were asked to read to an assembly of the student body on Wednesday afternoons. Despite the boys practicing and gaining praise for more flourishes in their oratorical presentations, the girls were also encouraged to express themselves in this public way. It is perhaps small wonder if it were difficult for the girls to suppress this developed and encouraged self-expression later, when they were expected to become demure, soft-spoken women, deferential to men.

By 1842, Emily was known about the school for her skill at compositions, and this early attention and praise for them probably went far toward planting the seeds of her desire to become a writer. One former teacher of hers at the time, Daniel T. Fiske, described the 12-year-old as "very bright," and her compositions as "strikingly original," mature in both thought and style, and revealed that her writing elicited not a little envy from her peers. He also described Emily as an excellent, conscientious student, but also "delicate and frail looking," and "somewhat shy and nervous."[1]

Emily Fowler, a classmate, commented favorably on the poet's contributions to a handwritten and hand-circulated student publication around the school, published by the more gifted students and called by them, *Forest Leaves*. The publication was written anonymously, but the handwriting of its authors was usually known well enough to give away their identities. The poet's distinctive, compact, and elegant handwriting of this period gave her away as the author of her compositions if the originality they exhibited did not. Fowler relates that Dickinson was "one of the wits of the school," and that her missives in these publications were simply "irresistible."[2]

It may be difficult to imagine how a bright, active student such as this middle-school and high school–aged girl would later retreat into her father's house and shut away her talent, as many might say. However, one must consider that school was not the only strong influence at work on the growing girl during these formative years. There were still few avenues of employment or opportunity for women interested in literature and writing at the time. The future was not nearly as promising for women of any talent as it was for men. Neither was the promise to survive into adulthood nor have a very long life for either gender secured. Death became a central concern to Dickinson in her early teens when she heard about the wives of professors she knew dropping dead like flies and she witnessed the traumatizing deathbed scene of young Sophia Holland.

Her return from her convalescence trip to Aunt Lavinia's after Sophia's death is marked by the occasion of meeting Abiah Root for the first time. She returned on a Wednesday, the day of student assemblies when students read their compositions aloud to the school. Climbing the stairs, it is said she spotted a new girl in the school who was wearing dandelions in her hair. The image imprinted itself on the soon-to-be poet's imagination, and she and Abiah Root became fast and good friends from that day forward. Although Abiah could never quite live up to the level of friendship Dickinson expected and needed from her over the years, she was an important companion and correspondent for the poet for some time.

Dickinson enjoyed Amherst Academy and never complained in any extant records about it, even when others did. The day began and ended in prayer and subjects were taught against an ecclesiastical background. Because the school was not endowed, teachers' salaries depended heavily on tuitions, so there was a high turnover in administration, faculty, and staff. Faculty members were often students themselves from nearby Amherst

College. Some students and families balked at the turnover and began transferring to other schools, but Emily stayed on, possibly in part due to the many days she had missed. The unusual arrangement of employing student faculty may have contributed a heightened energy and freshness to the instruction at Amherst Academy and perhaps even raised the bar in terms of expectations, since the teachers were not that much older than their young charges.

The connection with the college was also beneficial in that these young students sat in regularly on science lectures of the college faculty. Emily participated in this, notably climbing the stairs to the third floor with her classmates and listening in on the lectures given by an eminent geologist of the time, Professor Edward Hitchcock. At least three of his books, *Elementary Geology*, *Religious Lectures on Peculiar Phenomena in the Four Seasons*, and *Catalogue of Plants . . . in the Vicinity of Amherst*, influenced Dickinson's later writing.

HERBARIUM

One of the poet's Amherst Academy projects that survives to this day is a herbarium she prepared over several years while studying botany at the school. Dickinson loved hunting for plant specimens in the woods, fields, and hills of Amherst. She meticulously pressed them into her book, labeling them with their scientific names and numbers for class and order. Her herbarium, which is now kept at Harvard University, is an 11-by-13-inch leather book manufactured specifically for this purpose. It contains 400 to 500 specimens and includes plants found both in the wild and those cultivated in gardens or conservatories. In a letter to Abiah Root, who had left Amherst, Dickinson urges her to begin a herbarium if she has not done so at her new school because she would grow to treasure it.

The project no doubt began the poet's lifelong interest in flowers she would later cultivate for many years in the Homestead garden and in the small conservatory that her father built for her. It is interesting to note that in his papers on women's education, young Edward "Coelebs" Dickinson described botany as a subject that "refines and chastens" the women who study it.[3] In his quest to cultivate his daughter's refinement by encouraging her interest in botany into adulthood, the patriarch assisted in providing her with one of the subjects she is best known for now in her poetry—her observations of nature.

Dickinson's parents both appeared to believe that her field research in botany was good exercise for her health, because her herbarium shows evidence of expansion even over the periods of time when she was not allowed to go to school. Firsthand discovery of plants for her collection gave Dickinson not only a keen, close view of nature from the ground up, but it also stimulated her mind in the sciences, creating an awareness of differences among similar specimens and the ordering of these into various classifications. Her study heightened in her a naturalist's, objective viewpoint about the workings of nature, both the beautiful as well as the seemingly cruel and unpleasant. This ability to look at nature unflinchingly would influence the movement of her poetry away from the sentimental verse of her era. In addition, the poet appeared to view the collection for the memories each find stored for her. As biographer Alfred Habegger notes, this was the first collection of her lifetime; her hundreds of poems, kept in manuscript books of her own design, would be her second.

MOUNT HOLYOKE FEMALE SEMINARY

After the freedom of expression in composition class and the encouragement to explore the world in botany and geology classes at Amherst Academy, the strictures of all-female higher education at Mount Holyoke came as a departure for the poet that she never really fit into well. Dickinson attended Mount Holyoke from 1847–1848. One year was customary for middle class educated women of her time. The school was founded in 1837 by women's education reformer, Mary Lyon, as an institution with the primary intent of educating future missionaries. It did not yet award bachelor's degrees, but instead gave certificates of completion to those who finished their senior years. Since the majority of women at that time married and went home to raise families, it may not come as much of a surprise that most did not stay at school long enough to receive certificates.

Though it was still in its early phase of development by the time Emily Dickinson entered, Mount Holyoke was expanding in terms of enrollment and reputation. There were 235 students and 14 teachers[4] the year the poet moved the nine miles away from the house on West Street to South Hadley and settled into a room she shared with her cousin, Emily Lavinia Norcross.

The school days at Mount Holyoke were quite different from Amherst Academy, though surprisingly, the curriculum had not yet developed much beyond it. Nearly every half hour was scheduled for the students with activities of some kind beginning at six o'clock every day and going until the "retiring bell" at 8:45 in the evening. In a letter to Abiah Root,[5] Dickinson describes her daily schedule in the fall of 1847. Students were wakened at 6:00 A.M.; at 7:00 A.M. they ate breakfast. Study hours began at 8:00 in the morning, and at 9:00 A.M. Emily and the whole school met in the Seminary Hall for prayers. Classes were held at 10:15 and 11:00 A.M., and at noon students engaged in calisthenics for 15 minutes, then read for another 15 minutes until lunch at 12:30 P.M. From 1:30 until 2:00 P.M., Dickinson sang; and from 2:45 until 3:45 P.M. she practiced piano. At 3:45 she reported in at Sections, where students were to give an accounting of their day in terms of absence, tardiness, talking during silent study hours, having un-allowed guests in their rooms, or otherwise breaking the rules. At 4:15 P.M. the students once again filed into Seminary Hall, this time to hear a lecture from Miss Lyon. Dinner was at 6:00 P.M., and silent study hours followed from then until the bedtime bell at 8:45, with 9:45 P.M. being the hour when they were expected to be in bed and silent with lanterns out. Whereas just eight months earlier in her last year at Amherst Academy, Dickinson had written to Abiah asking her to forgive her glowing report of the school because she was always in love with her teachers at Mount Holyoke, the student confessed that her year at the Seminary was going to seem long. Homesickness, when she had time for it, struck Dickinson hard in South Hadley.

Mount Holyoke employed no housekeeping staff. The administrators were determined that domestic work built the women's characters and prepared them for the inevitable duty they would have to accept and bear all their lives. However, Dickinson's domestic duty was not too burdensome that fall—she reported to her friend that it involved transferring, washing, and drying the knives used at meals during the day.

Rather than provide a foundation against which to study the disciplines as it was at Amherst Academy, religion stood front and center at Mount Holyoke. Even more importantly, personal spirituality was analyzed and publicly scrutinized. Pressure from the administration, faculty, staff, and classmates all came to bear on individual students who had not yet submitted to a personal conversion. Students were separated into groupings of like-minded women for whom classes were held in order to convince them to move to the next level in their spiritual development. These included those with "a hope," for being saved; the "professors," or those who professed the faith as having been saved already; and a group with "no hope." Dickinson, with her refusal to go along with, or even pretend to go along with, what she did not believe in her heart, sat day after day with the no hope group, which grew smaller and smaller and endured more pressure as the year wore on.

Among other subjects, Emily took chemistry, physiology, and astronomy at Mount Holyoke. At the time, the school offered its strongest curriculum in the sciences. Not as much is known about Dickinson's student compositions at the Seminary, but seven surviving letters to Austin while she was there and three to Abiah Root reveal that she eventually came to speak fondly of the school and regarded its faculty as kind and caring.

Dickinson left and returned at least once during her year at Mount Holyoke due to illness, as all through her other school experiences, but concern over homesickness was apparently another reason. By May 1848 she wrote to Abiah Root that her father had sent Austin to bring her home for rest and medicine. Word had circulated back to West Street from her roommate Emily Norcross that Emily had a bad cough. She claims she fought with Austin about going home before the end of the term first with words, then by crying, but that Austin let her know that there would be no disobeying the man back at "headquarters."[6] While home was a welcome refuge for her, she dreaded the attention and treatment with medicines. While there, she kept up with her class by doing the work on her own. By the time she returned to South Hadley, Edward had notified her that this would be her last term at Mount Holyoke. His overprotection of his oldest daughter, or her longing for home—or both—had won out. By early August, 1848, at not yet 18 years of age, the poet's formal education had come to an end.

RELIGION

Dickinson's exposure to religious pressure did not begin or end at Mount Holyoke. The era in which she lived was ripe with revivals that swept through Amherst as they had many other New England towns at the time. Every few years visiting preachers came to towns and whipped up religious fervor with fire and brimstone sermons. Church committees prepared for these events by personally calling on those they knew to be unsaved, or by sending intermediaries from the person's family to talk to them about their faith and invite them to the revival. Pamphlets and leaflets were distributed, and the revival meetings were talked up at regular Sunday services.

During a revival meeting, the visiting preacher used his considerable oratorical skills to capture and hold the congregation's attention. Preachers used tactics such as telling sensational stories, relating long and detailed descriptions of sinners who resembled some of the people in the local community, describing graphic and fearsome depictions of hell in loud and thundering voices, and other methods to induce those listening to rethink their relationship with God. If the spirit moved them, whether out of guilt; a fear of death that surrounded them daily; community pressure; or what they believed to be a true moment of grace, the faithful would rise up from their seats, move forward, and announce to the world that they were saved.

Aside from Dickinson's mother, Dickinson's proud, practical family members took their time releasing their inhibitions and moving to this level of personal devotion and public surrender. Edward Dickinson, though a leader in local First Congregational Church affairs for many years, did not succumb to conversion until the revival of 1849–1850, when 70 members of the Amherst faithful "dropped" in one fell swoop. Lavinia converted at Ipswich Female Seminary, which she attended for one term. Abiah Root also pledged that she was saved. Only Austin and Emily held out for a time. Then Austin converted in 1855, shortly before marrying Susan Gilbert, and quite possibly for that purpose, because the poet's future sister-in-law had also converted years before at the same revival as Dickinson's father.

Her father gave her the gift of a Bible in 1844, which her letters and poems indicate she read. She listened to the Calvinist preachings of Rev. Aaron Colton at the First Church, which she heard from 1840 to 1853. Despite these influences and the pressures at Mount Holyoke in 1847–1848, the revivals in town, and the going along of family member after family member and friend after friend, Dickinson claimed that she alone stood in rebellion. The pressure had turned her further away from organized religion than ever, and by the early 1860s she refused to go to church at all. Instead, she preferred to stay home on the Sabbath and listen to the birds singing while she read and wrote letters to those she loved.

Many scholars read Dickinson's poetry today and see a soul searching for faith. Some see one with a highly developed sense of spirituality that would not be bounded by organized religion. Still others see a person who refused to believe in an unseen god; one with the clear-eyed view of a scientist and who would rather risk hell than be a hypocrite or pretend to believe in Bible stories. One fact about religion and Dickinson is clear to most of those who study her life or read her work—she pondered the concept of immortality and other spiritual questions all of her life.

EARLY FRIENDSHIPS

When some people today envision the poet Emily Dickinson, many see a shy, lonely woman working late into the night in her upstairs bedroom writing poem after poem about rather gloomy subjects. In truth, the poet enjoyed many friendships and acquaintances over her lifetime and had an active family life and household, which on many days could be anything but quiet. Her father's prominence in town demanded that his household be a center of activity. Eventually, Edward Dickinson would not only be a prominent attorney, leader of the First Congregational Church of Amherst, entrepreneur of the Amherst and Belchertown Railroad, and Treasurer of Amherst College, but he would also serve as a Massachusetts State legislator and a United States congressman. Clients, visiting lecturers and students at the college, politicians, governors, clergyman, and businessmen—were just a few of the kinds of people who regularly crossed the threshold of the Dickinson Homestead and required the entertaining efforts and skills of the Dickinson women. If she would choose to resist them later on, Emily Dickinson did not grow up a foreigner to the social customs and events of her day.

During her years at Amherst Academy, the young poet made many friends. She was part of a circle of five, in particular, with whom she traded secrets and jokes, shared compositions, music, and books, and enjoyed the normal comradery of girlhood. The group of five she identified in an 1846 letter were herself, Abiah Root (the girl with dandelions in her hair whom she met on the stairs), Abby Wood, Harriet Merrill, and Sarah Tracy. At one time, three of these had classical nicknames—Sarah was Virgil; Abiah was Plato; and Emily was Socrates. Added to these were other friends of various ages such as Mary Warner, Jane Humphrey and Jane's sisters Mary and Helen, Emily Fowler, Eliza Coleman, Jane Hitchcock, and Susan Gilbert. The intertwining circles of girls maturing in Amherst at the time included several who would distinguish themselves, including Helen Fiske, who was delivered by the same Dr. Cutler who delivered Emily Dickinson two months later. Helen Fiske would grow up to be the famous writer, Helen Fiske Hunt Jackson.

While Dickinson apparently found great fun associating with these friends, she did retreat to subdued silence on occasions when there were too many of them around at once, or when their merriment grew too loud or boisterous. Her penchant for witty and artful play in pairs and among smaller groups already displayed her preference for a quieter, more solitary way to spend her time. She enjoyed their company, but solitude was already exerting some of its sway over her, although it would not win her over for some time yet.

After leaving Mount Holyoke in 1848, Dickinson entered a social scene among young adults in Amherst that was probably one of the most active periods of interacting with friends that she would experience. Austin was attending Amherst College and was a member of the Alpha Delta Phi fraternity in his senior year. Emily formed several friendships with his male college friends and young women she met in overlapping circles, particularly enjoying intellectual discussions with them about literature and other matters. There were sleighing parties and valentines, sugarings, books traded and books read, whispered gossip in carriage rides, candy pullings, long walks, and mountain climbing. The young woman considering her future but not pressed financially to find employment as a teacher or governess as some women her age were doing at the time, performed her domestic duties as required at home, but she also enjoyed the company of men and women her own age. Though naturally shy, she was not yet afraid to seek out their friendship.

Ever protective of his eldest daughter who very much wanted to go out and visit with her and her siblings' friends, in 1850 Edward purchased a dog to accompany her when she might be alone in her walks about town or through the fields. The dog was a dark brown or black Newfoundland, a large breed, perhaps mixed with some St. Bernard. Dickinson named him Carlo. Suspected origins of the name vary from the dog in *Jane Eyre*, a novel Dickinson had read and loved, to the dog in another book she favored, Ik Marvel's *Reveries of a Bachelor*. In fact, Carlo was a common name for dogs in Amherst at the time; there were five dogs registered in town with that name in 1858.[7] Carlo, whom Dickinson would later call her "shaggy ally,"[8] would be her constant companion for over 15 years.

Among her young adult friends were Jane Humphrey, an old friend from Amherst Academy who returned to Amherst as preceptress for five terms and Emily Fowler, the woman who, as a girl, had praised Dickinson's *Forest Leaves* compositions. When Emily climbed Mount Holyoke with a group of friends on October 9, 1849, the group included John Laurens Spencer, a student at Amherst and a member of Austin's fraternity. Another friend from Austin's fraternity was George Henry Gould, who would later send her an invitation for a candy pulling, the back of which she would use to draft a poem about winter. James Parker Kimball gave her a copy of Oliver Wendell Holmes's *Poems*.

One of the friends who meant the most to Dickinson during this period was Benjamin Franklin Newton. Newton was nine years older than Emily and was not a member of her church but instead was a Unitarian. He was in town working as a law clerk for her father. Newton spoke with Dickinson about literature and writing and encouraged her in her literary aspirations. There was something about the freshness of his ideas, which came from outside the Calvinist orthodoxy she grew up with, as well as his high intelligence, and sense of morality that struck Dickinson to the core. He gave her a copy of Ralph Waldo Emerson's *Poems*, the first collection of Emerson's verses. The fact that Emerson was more known for his essays and speeches at the time shows that Newton had a sophisticated appreciation for the literature of the day and probably also had the insight to know that this book was a good choice for Dickinson.

For her part, Dickinson appears to have absorbed what Newton taught her about literature and took his advice about her writing to heart. He thought highly of her and of her talent and encouraged her to keep writing. Whether the relationship was a romantic one on either side is unknown, but Newton married someone else quite suddenly, and Dickinson never forgot his kind counsel. Newton may have been one of the first, if not the first, to encourage Dickinson in the notion that she could pursue her talent for writing on a serious, adult level. Many years after Newton's untimely death in March 1853, the poet wrote, probably about Newton, that she once had a tutor who had taught her immortality but going too close to it himself, had never returned.

Another literary friendship that began soon after Newton's marriage was with Henry Vaughan Emmons. Emmons's father was a judge in Maine when Emmons came to Amherst College as a student. Oddly enough, his grandfather had known Emily's grandfather; and the two young people shared many interests in common. His roommate was her cousin and friend, John Long Graves. One night Emmons and Emily took a ride *alone*, as the poet later emphasized to Austin, but whether their relationship went beyond friendship is not known. Emmons founded the *Collegiate Magazine* and became its editor. His essays spoke of poets who had to suffer to create their best art and how life is perfected by death, both ideas that echo strains of Dickinson's poetry. Whatever the ties that held their friendship may have been, they were apparently loose enough that after his graduation from Amherst College in 1854 Emmons became engaged to Susan D. Phelps of Hadley.

SUSAN HUNTINGTON GILBERT

Still another friend who would make a lasting impression and form a special relationship with the poet was Susan Huntington Gilbert. Susan was born about 10 miles away from Amherst in Old Deerfield, Massachusetts, on December 19, 1830, just nine days after Dickinson. Beginning then, their experiences would run different but parallel tracks, crisscrossing at important junctures all of their lives. Unlike Emily Dickinson, who enjoyed the security of having both parents and siblings living together in the same household in Amherst for many years, Susan, the youngest of seven children, became orphaned by 1841 and had to move to Geneva, New York, where she grew up under the care of her mother's sister, Sophia

Van Vranken. In 1846–1847, Susan went back east to attend Amherst Academy where she most likely knew Emily Dickinson, who was in her last year. In 1848–1850, Susan attended Utica Female Academy in Utica, New York. While she loved literature and liked to write, Susan's strongest skills were in mathematics, and she later went on to teach that subject in Baltimore, Maryland.

While living in Geneva, which is only nine miles from Seneca Falls where the first Women's Rights Convention was held in 1848, Susan witnessed firsthand Elizabeth Blackwell, who would become the first American female doctor, walk down the street to class at Geneva Medical College. Susan later attended Blackwell's graduation, which was a public affair recognized for the historical event that it was—even as it occurred that spring day in Geneva's Presbyterian Church. In those days, the air of central New York was charged with activism in both the women's suffrage movement and the abolitionist movement. Frederick Douglass came through town to lecture. Elizabeth Cady Stanton composed her historical speech, "Declaration of Sentiments," only a few miles away from where Susan Gilbert walked in a village overlooking the azure water of Seneca Lake.

By the time she returned to Amherst in the early 1850s, Susan and her sisters Mary and Martha came to live with their older sister, Harriet Cutler, and her unpleasant husband, William. The Dickinson siblings, particularly Austin and Emily, became reacquainted with Susan and Martha, who joined them in their exploits. Susan is described as having a strong and passionate personality, one befitting a woman who had survived a hard family life and entered adulthood in the homeland of women's independence. Among other characteristics, Susan was said to be intelligent, full of life, a good conversationalist with eclectic tastes, astute, and well read. She has also been described as arrogant, stern, and prone to angry outbursts. By contrast, her sister Martha was generally described as gentle and easy going.

In the fall of 1850, Austin was teaching in Sutherland, a few miles north of Amherst, for one term. Martha went to stay with the girls' wealthy brothers out in Michigan when their sister Mary died suddenly in childbirth. Emily and Susan remained close friends in Amherst, discussing books and writing and quite possibly also dreaming about their futures. In secret Austin had begun a romantic relationship with Susan and was courting her by letter.

Susan appeared at first to be headed for a different path than many nineteenth-century women. She seemed unimpressed with the traditional marriage and children scenario and even while her courtship continued with Austin, Susan packed up and moved to Baltimore, Maryland. She began teaching at the Archer's School for Young Ladies on what first appeared to those in Amherst as a whim. However, Susan needed the job. If she were interested in Austin, perhaps it was more due to the pleasure of being pursued than anything else. Their secret pact to each other to eat a chestnut wherever they were as the bell rang for vespers each evening was, no doubt, a sentimental gesture suggested by Austin. He probably found her independence a challenge compared to most of the women he knew—who perhaps sought out the company of one of Amherst's most prominent bachelors a little too readily. In keeping with their independent togetherness, Austin went to Boston to teach at the Endicott School, where hundreds of students crowded into the city classrooms, many of them the children of Irish immigrants.

Emily Dickinson found herself amid a strange emotional triangle. She missed Austin intensely when he was away in Boston. Letter after letter poured out of her to him, urging him to come home. Austin was her lifeline in recent years to a social life she enjoyed. In his absence, perhaps Emily could see that adulthood and its responsibilities were dawning on her contemporaries while she remained in her father's house with no obvious future plans. She remained friends with Martha Gilbert while their respective siblings were away working; once, Emily wrote to Susan on Martha's behalf when she was ill.

By early 1852, Emily's nearly constant letters to Austin and Susan commingled; one letter to Austin followed by another to Susan, each becoming more and more intense, passionate, and full of yearning. The poet's loneliness, accompanied perhaps with clarity about her own future, was beginning to settle in. The letters of this period suggest a last gasp of sorts for the old days. Dickinson even remarks to her brother that she wishes neither of them had to grow up. The poet was apparently seeing that she was neither going to be an independent woman outwardly breaking the mold of her society nor a wife, but just what she was going to be or do remained uncertain. Eventually, what came about took pieces from both of those scenarios.

When Susan returned to Amherst and Austin attended Harvard Law School, Emily depended more and more on Susan's companionship and their mutual interest in books and writing and their fondness for Austin. While other friends were getting married or were otherwise distracted from spending time with girlfriends, Susan became "Sister Sue" to Emily, and they became closer than ever. They lent each other books and discussed them. They shared interests in garden flowers and recipes; neither of them could tolerate the idea of housekeeping. They talked of their mutual love for writing and literature. Susan encouraged Emily in her writing even as she continued to keep journals, write poetry, stories, and essays herself. Perhaps Emily saw Susan as the advisor and encourager that Benjamin Newton had been. She was certainly someone who knew about books and took an active interest in Emily's writing, and she spoke her mind that Emily should pursue her writing. For her part, perhaps Susan shared her own ambivalence toward marriage and childrearing along with Emily and appreciated Emily's devotion and intellect. Perhaps the two conspired about how to write and publish as women of their time and lot in life. In a different time, perhaps they would have set up house together, Susan teaching math in school while Emily wrote poetry at home. Perhaps the two of them could have enjoyed intellectual discussions together in the evenings and sharing and critiquing each other's writing. But this was the middle of the nineteenth century, and the thought of setting out in a lifestyle so unconventional at the time probably never even entered into their minds. Perhaps the impulse in some ways led to what eventually did happen.

In 1853, Susan went to Manchester, New Hampshire, to visit her sister Mary's in-laws. On the train trip back to Amherst, Susan stopped off in Boston to meet Austin at the Revere Hotel. There, the couple pledged their love for one another and became engaged. When Susan returned to Amherst and told Emily about the engagement that was to be kept secret for the time being, Emily's next letters to Austin sound like she is making a congratulatory concession to him that he won over Susan, and she did not.

After several delays, mostly on Susan's part (perhaps again due to an ambivalence toward marriage), she and Austin were married on July 1, 1856, in Geneva, New York, at the Van Vranken home. Austin's plans to head west and set up a law practice were scrapped. Edward Dickinson enticed his son with a partnership in his now-successful Amherst practice and with a wedding gift of a new house built to Austin's specifications. The offer was too good for Austin to pass up.

"Sister Sue" was now legally so for Emily. Ironically, although Emily Dickinson would write more surviving letters to Susan Gilbert Dickinson over the course of her lifetime than to any other single correspondent, Susan would live right next door to the poet for the next 30 years.

NOTES

1. Qtd. in Sewall, *Life*, p. 342.
2. Qtd. in Habegger, "*Wars*," p. 164.

3. Qtd. in Habegger, *"Wars,"* p. 48.

4. Hitchcock, *Life of Mary Lyon*.

5. Dickinson letter to Abiah Root, October 21, 1847 (Dickinson, *Letters,* Johnson, 3 vols.).

6. Dickinson letter to Abiah Root, May 16, 1848 (Dickinson, *Letters,* Johnson, 3 vols.).

7. Margaret H. Freeman, "Carlo," in *An Emily Dickinson Encyclopedia*, ed. by Jane Donahue Eberwein (Westport, CT: Greenwood Press, 1998).

8. Dickinson letter to T. W. Higginson, February, 1863 (Dickinson, *Letters,* Johnson, 3 vols.).

Chapter 4

"FOR OCCUPATION - THIS - ": THE POET AT HOME

Neither marriage nor employment in the traditional women's occupations of the day as a teacher, nurse, or governess filled the bill for Emily Dickinson. By 1855 she found herself in her mid-twenties still at home with her sister and her parents. If she'd had any designs before this time to establish a household of her own independent of her father, she must have known that the prime years for this to happen were passing her by. Vinnie apparently had a steady stream of potential beaux, and at least one serious contender in a young man named Joseph Lyman. Emily, too, had her share of interested suitors—nonetheless, neither sister would marry. Some scholars place the reason for this squarely at the feet of one they describe as the sisters' overbearing and overprotective father. Others suggest that Emily and Vinnie's unusually high regard for both him and themselves resulted in their finding no one quite his match—nor their own.

During the years of active socializing with Austin's Amherst fraternity friends and others their age, Dickinson wrote a virtuoso valentine that was later anonymously published in the Amherst College literary journal, *The Indicator*. The addressee has been generally agreed upon to be George Henry Gould, the poor student editor of the journal who had invited her to the candy pulling. Vinnie denied years later that Edward stepped between Gould and Emily because of the man's poor economic status and uncertain future. Gould was probably not responsible for the valentine's publication. One story has it that the valentine was stolen from his desk and published by another editor on the journal. In letters to Abiah Root, Emily describes that while she was doing the dishes a young suitor asked her to go riding with him in the woods. Apparently, at that time she refused because of the work she had yet to do to help her mother. A lasting relationship with Gould never materialized, if it ever got going much to begin with.

There were other candidates who sought Emily's notice over the years. Even now speculation runs rampant. From what observers read into her poetry, there may have been at least one serious love affair gone awry that cut her deeply. Usually the men suggested for these roles are quite a bit older than she and are either married or widowed, or live far away from Amherst. That Emily may have preferred mature men or those who were otherwise out of reach is not beyond the realm of possibility. The older men would more likely have had the depth of wisdom she may have sought out in a match, and the married and distant ones may have insured for her that she would never kneel to take the marriage vow. Perhaps her intense feelings for Susan Gilbert confused her, or maybe Susan's addition into the family satisfied her. In any case, what many observers do not emphasize enough is the fact that although she was without a husband, Dickinson was not without love. Love's tribulations came to her as they do for everyone, those living with lifelong partners and those without.

Because the poet chose to write about the subject of love, its joys and its sorrows, does not mean that her romantic situation warranted the level of sensational treatment it has received over the years. Much of the identity seeking behind Dickinson's would- or wouldn't-be love affairs has fallen so low that it has reached the level of tabloid journalism—or at the very least, common town gossip. When all is said and done, the emotion that drove the poet to write is more important than that emotion's complicated conglomerate of causes, for there is rarely only one defining person or moment that precipitates great art. Endless speculation on the identity of any one individual at any given moment does more to separate readers from the poet and the poem than it does to bring them closer.

Both Emily and Vinnie took their loyalties to both of their parents seriously, as did Austin. One of Edward's legacies seems to have been instilling in his children an intense loyalty to the family equal, if not greater than his own. In one letter to Austin, Dickinson writes that the five of them prefer their own company, perhaps, more than any other because there is no other kind of person quite like them in the world. In another letter, Emily writes that she did not marry or move away so that she could continue to care for her mother, and she stayed at home to be near her father, who wished for her to stay near. With no other definitive evidence for her choice than this told in reflection many years later, perhaps this reasoning from Dickinson herself should be good enough explanation for the curious as to why the poet chose to remain at home and never marry. For women of her day, these were almost the only two choices available.

In any case, with Austin's marriage in 1856, the tight family grouping would solidify as all three siblings moved into adulthood. The only change would be the addition of Susan Gilbert who, despite her independence, also had an orphan's longing to reestablish a home and family. Austin's marriage, and the move of all six family members to Main Street, probably did more to affect the poet's work at the time than any other influence of those years.

RETURNING TO THE HOMESTEAD

Edward Dickinson's offer to build Austin a house for him and his new bride perhaps echoes what he would have wanted years before when Squire Samuel Fowler Dickinson had provided such a shaky start for him and Emily Norcross. What's more, the house was to be located right next door to the family Homestead built by Austin's grandfather, which Edward was now in the position to buy back. Edward's hard work and influence allowed him to buy back the entire house, both east and west halves, the two-and-a-half acre lot that it sat on, as well as the 11-acre meadow across the road. He paid $6,000 for everything to Samuel Mack, David Mack's heir who lived in Cincinnati, Ohio, and who needed the money after his father's death.

The Homestead, then, was finally free and clear and back in Dickinson hands. This must have been a moment of triumph for Edward. That he could also afford to set up his son as a partner in his law practice as well as build him a fine home on the lot next door as a wedding gift must have been even more satisfying for him. The new town Squire, as he was now called, Edward had corrected the wrongs done by his father on both accounts.

As construction of Austin's chosen design of an Italianate villa took place next door, renovations revamped the brick Homestead as well. Despite the Dickinson Yankee frugality of making use of existing walls and materials where possible, the extensive renovations may have cost Edward nearly as much as he paid for the house and property together. Entering through the gate from the road and up the walk to the main door of the Homestead, one first encountered a large main hallway that ran front to back and included a large, ornate, stairway. To the left, off the hall, were located a front parlor with a rear parlor behind that, and to the right side of the hallway were the library, the dining room behind that, and a pantry. The rear-ell area was removed and replaced with a service ell, two-stories high. It included a kitchen, washroom, and shed. The west wing gave way to a porch; and Edward added a small conservatory for Emily and her mother on the southeast corner of the house, off the library. The bedrooms were upstairs, Emily's being the one at the southwest corner with windows facing both Main Street below and toward her brother and Susan's house next door. Edward added an eight-windowed square cupola on top that provided a 360-degree view of Amherst, the Pelham Hills, and the Connecticut Valley. There was no question but that with this house, Edward was making a statement to the world that he had achieved his version of the American dream, and that the Dickinson family was here to stay.

In time, behind the Homestead there was a large barn complex that included carriage houses, stables, and a hen house. There was a shed for storing wood, and another, two-story shed for tools. One of the Dickinson's hired groundskeepers lived on the second-floor of the tool shed. In time, Edward had several workers in his employ, along with a full-time maid. This was the middle 1850s, and many Irish immigrants were arriving in town due to the Great Hunger (potato famine) occurring at that time in Ireland. Most, but not all, of Edward's hired workers would be Irish.

The layout of Austin's house was somewhat similar to the Homestead. Again, New England frugality came into play, as Edward built onto and around a rental cottage that was already present on the site. The cottage formed the service quarters in the back of the new house. The large entry hall out front opened to an ornate stairway. The parlor occupied the southwest corner on the ground floor. A veranda lined the exterior of the parlor, both on the south and west sides. Behind the parlor was the dining room. Behind that was a kitchen that had a unique passageway to place food and clean dishes inside a cupboard on the dining-room side. Behind the kitchen was a stairway to the upstairs of the service area. On the southeast corner of the hall at the front of the house was the library with double doors opening out onto a veranda. Susan's in-laws from the Homestead no doubt used this entrance, since it leads directly to the footpath that existed between the two houses. Behind the library was a bedroom with a dressing room and a shed-like area behind that. Upstairs on the west side was a large bedroom with the nursery behind that, followed by the maid's room. The nursery had an interior window along the back hallway so that the nurse or family could check in on a sleeping baby from the hallway without disturbance. On the east side were two other bedrooms followed by a loft. The square tower of the Italianate design rose at the south front of the house and could be reached by a small spiral staircase from the second floor. Austin's was the first house in Amherst for which its owners adopted the British custom of giving it a name. Austin named it The Evergreens, after his interest in landscaping.

By mid-October 1855, Emily wrote in a letter that the workers on the Homestead were putting up wallpaper, and the family would soon be leaving the West Street house where she had lived since she was nine years old. Her prediction came true the next month when she, Vinnie, and her parents, presumably with the necessary help, packed up all their belongings into wagons and carriages. The family moved around the corner, less than a mile, back to the large brick house built by her grandfather and where Emily had been born nearly a quarter of a century before.

A letter from Emily to Elizabeth Holland in January of 1856 describes how she felt about the move, which she apparently accomplished out of family duty but not out of any particular joy. Still, she makes fun of how lost she felt without knowing where her belongings were when they arrived. The image of Dickinson walking behind her bandbox (luggage) eastward and southward toward the rise on Main Street where the houses stood, brings to mind something like a funeral procession or a walk toward execution or some other kind of doomed fate. That walk from West Street to Main Street, no doubt with faithful Carlo loping at her side, may have been one of the longest in the poet's existence because of what it symbolized for her. Rather than becoming independent and moving forward, leaving home at this point in her life as many of her friends were doing or had already done, at 24, Emily was moving backward in time—not only to the house where she was born, but to the house where her father had been born as well.

This was Father's house, not Mother's. The necessary trappings of all that entailed with Edward's efforts at reestablishing the Dickinson legacy begun at the time of the colonies would be part of their new life in this home. Dickinson's tone in the letter about the move suggests that Edward would not consider anywhere else home except this particular house and property. However cool or stiff the poet may have thought the environment to be in the brick house her grandfather built, she could not have escaped knowing the importance that the move back into it had for her father and her family.

One of the feelings of dread she may have experienced as she went looking for herself early after the move was validated in her mother's sudden downturn in health as soon as they were settled. Vinnie and Emily had much more work to do in the new house. If Emily's letter is to be taken literally, all Mrs. Dickinson could do each day for a long period of time was sit in a chair and not get up.[1] Emily may have come to a realization that her future may lie in resigning to staying in her father's house and pursuing her writing with the helpful encouragement and constructive criticism of Sister Sue next door. However, if this were so, the long hard hours of necessary housekeeping duties she so disliked must have made the move seem like even this plan for herself was not going to work out.

For her part, Susan Gilbert Dickinson accepted Austin's decision to stay in Amherst and viewed it as the opportunity to launch into her own particular brand of setting up house and home. Being the best at this she possibly could be would be one of her life's projects. With Emily now conveniently living next door she could continue to write and share her interests in literature with her. Susan's wealthy Michigan brothers sent a healthy dowry that allowed her and Austin to furnish The Evergreens with the latest in furniture, light fixtures, wallpaper, draperies, and other decorative accessories. Susan set about selecting these items with creative zeal. In marrying Austin, perhaps she got what she most wanted, which may not have been a life with Austin in particular, but rather a life within an intact family. She now had a gracious brand-new home of her own where she could entertain guests whose intellectual or social connections she cared to cultivate. Edward Dickinson and Susan shared loyalties to the institution of family and family standing in a community after both surviving the risk of losing it. It may come as no surprise, then, that Susan not only liked Edward Dickinson and was said to understand him in ways many others did not, but that he reciprocated her fond regard. Like Edward had years before, Susan was willing to sacrifice her own desires about moving west to stay in Amherst and help build a family dynasty.

WILLIAM AUSTIN DICKINSON

With apparent readiness, the poet's older brother settled into his new life with Susan next door at The Evergreens. Not only had he been indulged by his father's offers of a law partnership and a brand-new home, but his wife was clearly one who would benefit his career by being the preeminent hostess of the town. Very soon it was The Evergreens, not the Homestead, that took on the role of hosting distinguished visitors in Amherst. Austin chose the original Italianate suburban villa plans, possibly from an 1842 architectural catalog, Cottage Residences, by Andrew J. Downing,[2] and oversaw its design by Northampton architect, Willam Fenno Pratt. Austin's later contributions to The Evergreens tended toward landscaping and art collecting. Outside, he supervised the landscape design of trees, shrubbery, and flowers. Inside, Austin began collecting original paintings, primarily landscapes that began adorning the walls of the parlor and library. Art collecting took Austin on trips to galleries and auctions in cities for many years. Among his many purchases included a very large land-scape, *Norwegian Scenery, with Bears* (1842) by Hans Frederik Gude that still hangs in The Evergreens and much later, *Winter Scene with Fox* (1882) by C.H. Shearer. Susan shared this interest with her husband, purchasing art including John F. Kensett's *Sunset with Cows* (1856) and Arthur Parton's *Woodland Scene: Oaks at Old Shokan* (c. 1876).[3] Adorning the mantle in the parlor in prominent display was a striking and sensual sculpture study by Canova, *Cupid and Psyche*. Visitors to The Evergreens in later years when Susan's and Austin's marriage was suspected to be strained must have looked at the sculpture with a touch of irony and wonder.

Though he began making a living and a name for himself in the community at this time, Austin and Emily had been very close as children and remained so, at least through the early days of his marriage if not longer. The poet once wrote to him when he was away at college that she wished they could be children again, talking for hours late at night in the kitchen as they used to do or running through the woods exploring. Austin had toyed a bit with writing, though never as seriously as his sister or his wife, but he did keep a faithful diary for many years. He and the poet shared jokes about their parents, plotting how to sneak popular books they both wanted to read past their father as they both sat in the parlor, "in state," as the poet characterized it. Austin was aware that Emily wrote, but perhaps not that she took her writing as deadly seriously as she did. Unlike the wild streak the poet exhibited in the daringness of her poems, Austin liked to ride horses fast down Main Street, galloping past her bedroom window on his way to work at the law office. His sister often joined in his merriment by waving a salute out the window to him as he passed.

Austin's interest in landscaping only began with The Evergreens. In what might be viewed as blending the civic responsibility of his father with the artistic leanings of his sister, Austin later went on to contribute to the town of Amherst by being influential in the planting of several trees around town, establishing Wildwood Cemetery, and Amherst Common. He came to know landscape designer Frederick Olmsted, who designed New York's Central Park, and ask for his counsel on several of these projects as well as the landscaping of buildings at Amherst College. He succeeded his father as treasurer of the college in 1873, was instrumental in the building of the new Congregational Church across Main Street from The Evergreens, and seemed to grow, like his mother, more reserved in public as he grew older.

Many said Austin was the most arrogant of all of the Dickinsons, but his arrogance may have come more from a spiritual searching and dreamy longing for beauty in life and his place in it than from a sense of entitlement or superiority. Just the same, unlike his father who had known hardship and worked to recover Samuel Dickinson's defamation of the family name, Austin never had that kind of outward struggle. Perhaps he came to think that because of that he deserved the comfortable life he enjoyed without necessarily having to earn it. Idolized by his mother and two younger sisters, Austin grew up enjoying being the center of female attention. Perhaps it was this expectation that would cause problems in his marriage with his independent wife later on.

LAVINIA NORCROSS DICKINSON

From the poet's description in letters, she and her sister Vinnie could hardly have been more different, yet at the same time they could hardly have been closer. Vinnie enjoyed the orderliness of housekeeping, and though she was nearly as educated as Emily (she attended Ipswich Female Seminary for one term past Amherst Academy), it was Austin and Susan, not Vinnie, to whom the poet turned when she wanted to discuss books. Just as Father had asked her to do when they began school as young girls, Vinnie never let go of her protective attitude toward her older sister. She admired Emily's need to think and respected her wish to be alone with her books and papers. In some ways, Vinnie took on somewhat of a maternal role in the household, caring for Mother and Father, respecting Emily's thinking time, and finding her own happiness through nurturing her family's needs.

Vinnie kept a rather cryptic diary starting in 1851 and lasting only a few days into 1852. The diary is more a log of activities than any outpouring of secrets or emotions. Nevertheless, the diary has been useful to scholars in piecing together actions and whereabouts of the family.

To Emily's dislike, Vinnie enjoyed cats and had several of them around the Homestead. She was a good mimic and was more forthright and direct in her dealings with people than perhaps anyone else in the immediate family, except perhaps Susan. Vinnie was not afraid to speak her mind in the village while shopping or at the door of the Homestead when guarding her sister's coveted privacy. Vinnie was practical, hard working, and comfortable with her place in the world. When her most serious suitor Joseph Lyman visited, she would hold him in her arms. Lyman once described her ardor in sitting on his lap, unpinning her long chestnut hair and tying it around his neck, kissing him passionately. In the evenings, he related, she would pull up a red ottoman beside his chair, lay a book on his lap, and read, clinging to his arm.

Whether Lyman found Vinnie too clinging or not is hard to say, but after entertaining serious thoughts of marrying her, he married someone else after moving south to New Orleans. Lyman kept in touch with the Dickinsons (he knew both sisters) over the years, and his letters to his fiancée suggest a lingering interest in them and fond memories of Vinnie. On the eve of his marriage, he wrote that if she had not so loved her roses, house, and family so possessively, he might well have married her. He was afraid she would miss all of these things, so he had left her there with them when he moved south.

Lyman's comments are interesting, given that Vinnie was the more outgoing of the two Dickinson daughters. The family preference for its own home and kind was evident even in her, and early on. Years later, appreciating her sister's lifelong work and devotion to the family, the poet would summarize her character by calling her both a soldier and an angel.

THE POET AT HOME

Though they still shared many talks and consultations about writing and reading, Susan Dickinson's new project of furnishing The Evergreens was a distinctly different one than Emily's. In 1856, while Susan had a whole house to decorate, provide for, and otherwise take up her creative energies, the Homestead was mostly a chore to Emily, who performed her duties as quickly as possible and then retreated upstairs to her bedroom as soon as she was able. Jean Mudge[4] has argued that the move back to the Homestead in 1855 marked the beginning of the poet's habit of serious writing, and it is likely that this was the case. Looking out her south window at the activity on Main Street below, the poet could eavesdrop on and ponder the social scene of Amherst and the world. Looking westward toward her brother's house, along the footpath once called wide enough for two who love, she could keep an eye and ear on the family scene happening in that direction. The stairwell outside her room probably channeled voices and noise upstairs that kept her aware of what was happening in the immediate family, and the front gate and door, just below her window, gave her a bird's-eye view before anyone else in the house of who was dropping by to call. Far from being shut away from everyone and out of touch, the location of Emily's room provided her with an observation post that kept her connected with the outside world even as she retreated from it for the privacy necessary to begin her life's work. It was the best room in the house for the poet to write in, and write she did.

Among other things, her room consisted of a sleigh bed and a cherry writing table about eighteen inches square. The table had a smooth, wood-grained writing surface and one small drawer with a pull-ring handle. The drawer pulled in and out smoothly and easily. The legs were straight and smooth in the Shaker style. Her chair was a painted Hitch-cock. Along the west wall underneath a mantle, the room was warmed by a fireplace that later housed a Franklin stove. Eventually, on the walls the poet would hang pictures of writers George Eliot, Elizabeth Barrett Browning, and Thomas Carlyle. Other images that restoration scholars still investigate may have included a Currier and Ives drawing of Windsor Castle, a painting by her mother, and other pictures of family and friends. Hyacinths crowded the windowsills, and the poet enjoyed tending to them in their various stages of development during the changing seasons. Along one wall sat a good sized four-drawer cherry bureau, the bottom drawer of which contained scraps and beginnings of what would eventually become a body of work so original that it would become prized one day as among the best poetry the world had ever seen. The day when the poet's bureau, writing table, and chair would be deemed priceless treasures and be locked away for preservation at the Houghton Library at Harvard University was still in the distant future.

PORTFOLIOS

According to editor Ralph W. Franklin, in the summer of 1858, the poet began taking stock of the many poems and drafts she had accumulated both before and after the move to the Homestead. At this time, she started organizing her collection, much as she had done years earlier with her herbarium. Her organizing principle remains unknown to this day. It does not appear to be chronological nor necessarily by subject matter or imagery, though scholars such as Eleanor Elson Heginbotham and others suggest some kind of interior connections among the poems may have caused the poet to group them together. For whatever reason, and under whatever rubric she set in her mind, Dickinson began re-copying poems she liked in ink onto fine stationery, and destroying worksheets and drafts. As she organized, she turned a small sheet of pre-folded stationery over on its side, with the creased edge on the left, like a book. On the four sides of the folded sheet starting with the top page, she wrote poems, one after the other, usually separating them from one another with a horizontal line. When she had completed a number of these four-sided sheets, she put them together, not by inserting them one inside the other, but by stacking the creased edges together and poking a needle through them from front to back, once toward the top and once equidistant toward the bottom. Through the holes she sewed a thin cord. She threaded it from back to front and tied the pages together in a single knot toward the center of the front page. There were no covers on her manuscript books, no titles to the booklets or poems, no dates, and no page numbers.

Presumably, stacking rather than inserting the folded sheets together allowed her to make changes to a single poem without having to copy over an entire packet. She could simply untie the packet, remove the folded sheet or sheets that contained the poems she wished to change, rewrite those lines, and thread the packet back together. Dickinson continued to make markings on the poems suggesting word variants and other revisions even after they were bound in booklets, but the revisions didn't happen in the booklets until later. The earliest booklets seem to be an attempt at collecting finished copies; variants do not appear on them.

Like her herbarium with its hundreds of specimens, this collection was not a short-term affair. Between 1858 and 1865, Dickinson sewed together 40 portfolios of poems and gathered 10 unsewn sets of them together. Combined, this amounted to about 800 poems. She sent hundreds of others in the over 1,000 letters she wrote that still survive. While Vinnie, Susan, and several of her friends and correspondents knew she was writing poetry, no one knew in her lifetime that Dickinson had put together a corpus so immense. Though it was by no means the only place she wrote, also working on backs of wrappers in the kitchen and pantry, or at another small table in the dining room, it appears the upstairs bedroom in the Homestead is where the poet wrote the bulk of her life's work.

RALPH WALDO EMERSON

Perhaps it is no accident that Dickinson began making her booklets (also called manuscript books, fascicles, or packets in Dickinson studies) soon after Austin and Susan hosted a literary giant at The Evergreens, Ralph Waldo Emerson. In her "Annals of The Evergreens,"[5] a memoir written for her children about the guests and times in their childhood home that obviously takes pride in the accomplishment of entertaining well-known guests, Susan Dickinson describes the first of what she claims were several visits by Emerson. She explains that she had read and admired his work for so long that it nearly completely unnerved her to think that this godlike figure would actually be eating and sleeping in her home. It is interesting to note that she dates Emerson's first visit as occurring in 1857. The date indicates that within only a year or so of their marriage and the building and furnishing of The Evergreens, Austin and Susan were already a power couple in town, in a position to entertain figures from the top echelon of academia, literature, and society. This quick maneuvering must have relieved some of the pressure to perform this service at the

Homestead. Susan's youthful and independent ambition to accomplish her new project to an excellent degree apparently worked quickly and garnered wide attention in town. The poet's mother's household and hosting efforts supported her husband's law practice and his connections to politics and the college but perhaps she was not particularly progressive in her approach to social matters. Unlike her, Susan channeled her ambition and abilities into actively establishing the premiere household in town that everyone who came to Amherst would want to visit. In other words, while Edward's wife played her part out of duty when she was not always feeling particularly well, Susan appears to have played hers out with gusto and with her own individual stamp of originality.

Even to this day, some locals in Amherst have an attitude about Susan that seems to suggest that her ambition, particularly as a female, was too bold and ill placed in their small New England town. It is noteworthy that Susan's description of meeting Emerson emphasizes that Austin did more of the talking. Susan describes the anticipation of meeting Emerson as something like preparing to meet God, to which Emily commiserated by describing his impending arrival as seemingly coming from the place where dreams are born. On encountering his quiet manner in her home, Susan relates in her memoir that she fell silent in awe and was glad that Austin was able to carry on the conversation.

There is no evidence thus far to suggest whether Emily Dickinson did or did not meet Ralph Waldo Emerson when he visited her brother's home next door. It is tempting in these times to think a meeting may have occurred and that Dickinson's intense response to it may have been to begin putting together her booklets in what Emerson called in his essay, "New Poetry,"—"portfolios."[6] In that piece, he argues that there was a growing preference by Americans in the new democracy to keep private or hand-circulated "portfolios" of their writing rather than submit their works for publication in books. Though there is no evidence of a meeting, it is difficult to imagine Susan, Austin, and Emily not engaging in excited talk about Emerson's visits before and after they occurred, and for this literary giant's proximity in her world not to influence Dickinson and her work practice in some meaningful way.

* * *

During their years in The Evergreens, with Austin's involvement in the town's civic development and the college, his taking over the post of treasurer of Amherst College from his father in later years, and Susan's creative efforts at entertaining, the couple hosted many notable guests. These included politicians such as Governor Alexander Hamilton Bullock of Massachusetts; architects such as landscape designer Frederick

Olmsted; abolitionist lecturers such as Wendell Phillips; and writers such as Harriet Beecher Stowe and Frances Hodgson Burnett. These prominent guests and many other family and friends visited a house at the end of a well-worn footpath just 200 yards away from the Homestead, a house well known and readily visible to the poet from her two westward windows. For those who believe the poet was completely cut off from the world when she worked at home alone in her room, visits by literary notables next door provide windows of opportunity for influence. These windows remain open between the houses with many, thus far, unanswered questions.

NOTES

1. Dickinson letter to Elizabeth Holland, c. January 20, 1856. (Dickinson, *Letters*, Johnson, ed., 3 vol.)

2. See Note no. 12 in Mary Elizabeth Kromer Bernhard, "Mary Landis Hampson: Guardian of the Dickinson Universe," *Emily Dickinson Journal* 8, no. 1 (1999): pp. 24–35.

3. St. Armand, *Emily Dickinson and Her Culture*, p. 310.

4. Mudge, *Emily Dickinson and the Image of Home*.

5. Susan Gilbert Dickinson, "Annals of The Evergreens," *Dickinson Electronic Archives*, http://www.iath.virginia.edu/dickinson/susan/tannals.html.

6. Ralph Waldo Emerson, "New Poetry," *The Dial* vol. 1 no. 2 (1840): pp. 137–58.

Chapter 5

"HER TRAVELS DAILY BE":
TRAVELING NEAR AND FAR

Contrary to popular belief, Emily Dickinson did leave Amherst several times during her life. Few readers disagree that she traveled further than most within the realm of her poetry. Thoreau states in *Walden* that you don't have to travel far physically to travel far mentally. In establishing her workroom upstairs in the Homestead, Dickinson seems to have lived out that creed much as Thoreau did in building the cabin on Emerson's land at Walden Pond.

There used to be a popular T-shirt sold in Concord, Massachusetts, that read: "Thoreau Went Home on Weekends," meaning that even while he spent his chosen two years and two months at the cabin, the writer was not the isolated hermit many imagine him to be today. Thoreau maintained active ties and connections to his family and friends and to the village as a whole. The adage "no man is an island" applies to both of these literary travelers, male and female. Although neither Dickinson nor Thoreau made world tours to exotic lands in order to write travel books, as did writers such as Mark Twain, or made westward journeys to Colorado and California like Samuel Bowles or Helen Fiske Hunt Jackson,[1] the travels they did make suited them and their purposes well enough. For her part, from her first stormy, hurried carriage ride with Aunt Lavinia through the woods heading to Monson when she was two years old to the train ride home from Boston in 1865, Emily Dickinson traveled for four principle reasons: to visit family, to go to school, to please her father, and to regain her health.

The problem with the necessity of depending on written records to narrate a life is the indeterminable gaps in a life that written records do not capture. Certainly, Dickinson's first trip to Monson with her Aunt Lavinia Norcross when she was small would not have been her last. As the seat of her mother's branch of the family, Monson would have been the destination for several visits that occurred with some degree of regularity. This would also be true for the locations of her other extended family, on both sides, who lived in villages neighboring Amherst or the surrounding area. For example on one trip in 1838, Emily, then age eight, and her sister were left at Enfield with their Dickinson relatives while the girls' parents went on to Boston. On another trip, to Middletown, the poet and her sister visited their friend, Eliza Coleman. As a teenager, the poet's trip to South Hadley to attend Mount Holyoke in 1847 seems uneventful enough, emotional as it must have been for her (as for any college student today) with the anticipation of roommates, new classes, and schedules. She must have wondered what it would be like and whether or not she could measure up to the school's expectations and her expectations of herself. In one letter, she explains how she had worried about passing examinations there that would determine her placement. If she did poorly, she would be sent home. She needn't have worried. Once she made the relatively short trip to Mount Holyoke Female Seminary from Amherst, there is little evidence that she went much beyond the campus gates apart from a carriage ride or two.

DR. JOSIAH AND ELIZABETH HOLLAND

Dickinson also visited Springfield, Massachusetts, on two occasions that scholars are aware of—in early September 1853 and on September 19–20 in 1854. On these trips, she accompanied her sister Lavinia to the home of Dr. Josiah Holland and his wife, Elizabeth. Dr. Holland left the medical profession and became engaged in writing and editing. The Dickinsons met him through Samuel Bowles; Holland worked with Bowles as a literary editor at the *Springfield Republican* and became one of the best-known essayists in the country and an editor at Scribner's. Dr. Holland received an honorary degree at Amherst College commencement in 1851, probably largely due to Edward Dickinson's influence. When he visited the West Street house again in June of 1853, he invited the two Dickinson sisters to visit him and his wife in Springfield.

The visits were short, but apparently memorable for the poet. She hit it off with Elizabeth Holland, especially, and Mrs. Holland became the fortunate recipient of dozens of uninhibited, telling letters from the poet over the years that followed. Perhaps Elizabeth reminded her of her Aunt Lavinia in temperament. In all, the poet sent her over 30 poems. The visits to the Hollands in Springfield, and the long talks with them at the hearthside, are the best-recorded, and possibly the only overnight trips the poet made to visit friends. Father was cautious to make sure both sisters went together.

Besides these travels to nearby towns for family, friends, and school, written records show that Dickinson visited Boston more than once and made an eventful trip to Washington, D.C., Mount Vernon, and Philadelphia in 1855. As he did with so many of his daughter's actions, Edward Dickinson played a prominent role in all of Emily's travels. She did not travel without his approval. Though Edward was not a big traveler himself by today's standards, he made several trips through the years in his career in law and politics. He particularly liked cities and thought that they had a stimulating effect on folks from small towns; he considered them especially good for shaking off bouts of melancholia. Eventually, Edward would see his eldest daughter visit three of the four major cities along the East Coast. As the father of a genius poet now known so well for her preference for home, it is perhaps ironic that Edward is responsible for most of his daughter's trips away from Amherst. In fact, Edward eased travel to and from Amherst for everyone in a way that shows his influence even to this day.

AMHERST AND BELCHERTOWN RAILROAD

One of Edward's shining achievements in Amherst was his success in establishing the Amherst-Belchertown branch railroad line. Edward had wanted a line to come through Amherst for some time and had made several previous attempts to make it happen. In 1850 he tried again when a railroad reached as close as nearby Palmer from New London to the south. Edward proposed a line that would extend from Palmer to Montague and run through Belchertown and Amherst, but he was only able to finance a branch line. With Luke Sweetser and Ithamar Conkey, Edward incorporated the Amherst-Belchertown line and began raising money for its construction. Amherst residents all across town were encouraged to buy shares over the resistance of local farmers such as Thomas Hastings of South Amherst who didn't want the tracks dividing up his land. Momentum built in Edward's favor when he kicked in so much of his own money, and by 1853 the new line was completed.

That summer, a large group of people from New London stepped aboard the A&B train and traveled north, disembarking in Amherst. In a letter to Austin, Emily describes the scene of celebration from her secluded observation post in Professor Tyler's woods as her father greeted the New Londoners and led the visitors around town. Already she was showing that she did not like the limelight that puffed up her father with his own sense of self-importance, but neither did she want to miss out on the opportunity to watch him glow. It was Edward's hope that the line would bring additional revenue to Amherst, but as a branch line that revenue did not materialize, and Edward and others ended up losing money on the enterprise in the long run. Nevertheless, in many ways, it is still Emily Dickinson's father people must credit today when they step aboard Amtrak at Amherst Station and step off at Penn Station, New York City, or even when they visit Amherst and hear the low moan of the whistle as a train slowly passes through town.

WASHINGTON AND PHILADELPHIA

Two years after he brought the railroad to town, and the same year they would move back to the Homestead in the fall, Edward Dickinson wanted Emily to see Washington, D.C., where he served in the Thirty-third Congress of the United States. Edward was a member of the House of Representatives from the Tenth District of Massachusetts. With only a few weeks left to complete his lame-duck term, Edward appears to have planned the trip as an educational experience for Emily and perhaps as a chance to make some final connections in Washington's social scene before he left office. For a similar trip in 1854, in which he took Mrs. Dickinson, Austin, and Lavinia to the capital, Emily's father allowed her to stay home at the house on West Street. Interestingly, Susan Gilbert stayed at the house with her. Cousin John Long Graves, then a student at Amherst College, provided the requisite male protection. The next year, with Susan and Martha Gilbert due to return to Amherst from a trip, Emily was not happy about leaving, but she dutifully survived the long journey south and checked in with Father and Vinnie at the Willard's Hotel on February 10, 1855.

Willard's was the hub of the social and political scene in Washington at the time. The hotel was located at 1404 Pennsylvania Avenue SW, just a few short blocks from the White House. During the Civil War, Nathaniel Hawthorne called Willard's more the center of Washington and the Union than either the White House or the State Department. Abraham Lincoln was a frequent guest, staying there while he was in Congress and again before his inauguration as President. It is said Lincoln conducted official business from his room while staying there, such as making Cabinet appointments and working on his first Inaugural Address. General Ulysses S. Grant became a patron of Willard's during the Civil War, apparently enjoying socializing in the lobby, in particular. From this activity, Grant coined the Washington term still used in the early twenty-first century, *lobbyist*.

That Emily Dickinson was thrust into such an active, high-profile environment for three weeks seems almost unfathomable to those who know the volumes of intimate, interior poetry she would write in her bedroom a few years later. There is little known about what the sisters saw while in Washington. Austin remained home with Mother, and the sisters wrote to him, but most of these letters do not survive. From other letters, we know that Emily did not appreciate having to dress to impress (the fancy clothes made her feel like a peacock, she says in one letter), and not surprisingly, she did not find the constant schedule of one social gathering after another very enjoyable, even to the point of becoming ill for a time. Apparently, she recovered in time to join Vinnie in talks and walks with the other women who accompanied the men to Washington. At least one report from another government official's family member she met in the city, Mrs. James Brown of Alabama, describes Emily as big-hearted and warm with delicate tastes. Apparently, while she suffered under the discomfort of being put on display for her father, Emily rose to the occasions he required and represented Massachusetts in the Washington social circle as best she could for the three weeks they were there.

Evidence of one sightseeing stop near Washington does survive, and that was a visit to George Washington's home, Mount Vernon, which had just been opened to the public for touring. Visitors had to get there by taking a boat across the Potomac. Perhaps it is fitting that a poet who would later become so associated with her home should visit what would become the second most-visited historic home in the United States (next to the White House). She and Washington shared a love for their respective homes. Washington could have been Dickinson speaking about the Homestead a few years later when he said that he'd rather be at Mount Vernon with a friend or two than at the seat of government amid officers of the State and the powers of Europe. He lived at Mount Vernon for 45 years and while there he expanded the house several times and added the cupola, among other characteristics. Observers have wondered whether Edward may have adopted the cupola for the Homestead from his impressions of Mount Vernon.

In a letter to her friend Elizabeth Holland, Dickinson comments on Washington's marble tomb, that they walked hand-in-hand by it without speaking. She says that they paused briefly but were made no more wise or sad by seeing that "marble story."[2] Interestingly, she warms in her telling about the house, in particular raising the door latch that Washington must have raised when he went home one last time. She says that she could spend a long day indeed telling of her visit to Mount Vernon if it wouldn't bore Mrs. Holland, and that maybe she will do that when she gets back home. From the pleasant spring day she describes to the promise to tell more in person on her return, the trip to Mount Vernon appears to be one that Dickinson enjoyed. The juxtaposition of the images of Washington's tomb and his home and Dickinson's reference to Washington coming home one last time will not be lost on readers of Dickinson's poetry with its frequently interchangeable metaphors of home, tomb, and death. Leaving the bustle of the busy city hotel for this pleasant retreat to Washington's country mansion on a sunny spring day in Virginia must have been a welcome change for her. Her mentioning of the door latch is an intimate detail that suggests she shared a bond of familiarity with anyone who valued his or her home above all else.

After three weeks in Washington, Edward accompanied his daughters to Philadelphia, where he left them to visit with their second cousin, Eliza Coleman, who lived on Nineteenth Street below Chestnut. Edward returned to Amherst while Emily and Vinnie stayed on with the Colemans for another two weeks. Eliza's father, Lyman, had been Emily's German teacher, and now he was the leader of the Presbyterian Academy in Philadelphia. Though they were still in a city, now the Dickinson daughters were out of a hotel environment and back in a private home.

Again, not much is known about what the Dickinson daughters may or may not have seen while they were in this city. Until, and unless, more documents are uncovered about their stay, the principal event that is known is about Dickinson's apparently hearing Reverend Charles Wadsworth preach at the Arch Street Presbyterian Church. Wadsworth was a well-known and effective speaker. His voice was deep and powerful but reserved and controlled, and he used language with intelligence, grace, and humor. His manner was effective enough and known widely enough that it made an impact on unbelievers such as Mark Twain, a man who could give a talk or two himself and was not easily impressed. Apparently Wadsworth made such an impression on Emily that she would later seek out his counsel when she arrived back home in Amherst. Certainly, his flair for language was an attraction to writers of his day. There is some speculation that the poet's correspondence with Wadsworth turned romantic and clandestine, and that secret letters were passed to this married man, possibly through the Hollands. Definitive evidence of this, however, as with other possible romantic relationships of the poet, remain elusive and inconclusive.

When Emily and Vinnie arrived home, the move back to the family Homestead from the West Street house was only a few months away. Though it would not be the last time she ever left the town limits, as far as is known, this five-week trip with her father and her sister was the only one Dickinson ever made in her father's company and at his special request to expand her view of the world.

BOSTON

Emily Dickinson visited Boston several times in her life, and each time she did it was for matters related to her health and well-being. Edward began his "city cure" for her melancholia (which he also prescribed for his wife at times) when Emily was 13 years old. This first Boston trip followed her childhood trauma of witnessing her friend, Sophia Holland's, deathbed scene in 1844. Young Emily stayed away nearly a month on this trip, from middle May to early June, residing with her Aunt Lavinia and Uncle Loring Norcross, who ran a dry-goods store. They lived at Twenty-five McLean Street in the West End of the city with their young baby daughter Louise and Emily's uncle, Joel Warren Norcross. The first visit in Boston included time visiting her great aunt on Edward's side, Lucretia Bullard, and her husband, Reverend Asa Bullard. The Bullards lived close by the Norcross's, and Reverend Bullard then worked for the Massachusetts Sunday School Society where he edited the influential children's Sunday school periodical, *The Sabbath School Visiter*. The visit concluded with a few days with the poet's uncle, William Dickinson, and his family in Worcester.

Little is known about what Emily may have seen on this trip that was designed to perk up her spirits following Sophia Holland's death. However, it is known that, as he had years before with her mother, Edward strangely recommended that Emily visit the State Lunatic Hospital when she was in Worcester. While Edward apparently heard discussion about improvements in the care and facilities of the hospital in Worcester when he served in the Massachusetts state legislature and may have shared the progress and discussion of this issue with his family, the suggestion to visit the facility still strikes an odd chord to twenty-first-century readers. Whether she actually went to the facility or merely passed by is unknown. However, the message sent by his suggestion to visit the hospital as part of the city cure, which he sent his female loved ones on, seems barely veiled. It seemed to say: There are places where people can go if they cannot manage to get a grip on their emotions, including melancholia.

It is interesting how, beginning when Emily was very small, Aunt Lavinia was so frequently the one to whom Emily was sent when she was in emotional distress or need. This goes some distance in explaining why Emily became so attached to Aunt Lavinia's daughters, her cousins Fanny and Loo later on. While the Norcross cousins transcribed the poet's letters to them later in life, and the originals were presumably destroyed, the resulting transcriptions show a woman who writes to them as though they were still children when they were actually grown up and middle aged. The loss of the original letters may make the accuracy of their transcription remain open to some debate—although, so far there has been little, if any, challenge to their authenticity. The intimacy and playfulness in her letters to the Norcross cousins suggests an early, relaxed relationship of honesty, trust, and sharing of one's emotions on the Norcross visits that Emily perhaps did not enjoy in quite the same way at home.

Another example of what was expected at West Street manifests when Father writes to Emily in Boston of Vinnie's courage in enduring the days without her. He writes that Vinnie is independent, doesn't speak of Emily, and means to stick it out. Translated, this means that Vinnie misses her sister as she would miss a part of herself but that she is following what is expected of her in the household in terms of not letting her emotions get the best of her, even to the point of not speaking of her sister at all. Edward's letter is very telling about the emotional climate of the siblings' upbringing, since this brave young soldier holding in her emotions about missing her sister was only 11 years old at the time. Clearly, keeping a stiff upper lip was expected of both the females, protected as they were, and the males in Edward and Emily Norcross Dickinson's household.

If Edward is regarded as overprotective, particularly of the women of his family, the irony that it was he who sent Emily away at age 13 to recover her spirits in the large city of Boston continues when one considers that the young girl apparently traveled there alone. Her return trip involved riding the Boston and Worcester Railroad and then the Western Railroad between Worcester and Palmer before catching a stagecoach between Palmer and Amherst (Edward's A&B railroad had not yet been built). Before she left Worcester, Edward wrote her a letter that is also telling of his perhaps odd means of protecting her. In the letter, he cautioned her to be careful on the return home and to make sure she be careful when getting off the train cars "lest they should start, and throw you down and run over you."[3] Under Aunt Lavinia's care and the change of scenery, young Emily's spirits gradually improved so much that she was able to return to Amherst Academy immediately on arriving back in town in June.

The poet paid another visit to her Norcross relatives in Boston in 1846. On this trip she was 15 and was, apparently, accompanied by Vinnie. She wrote to her beloved school friend Abiah Root perhaps the lengthiest description of any of her travels.[4] In this correspondence, Emily describes to Abiah that she had been ill much of the spring and summer, and that Father and Mother thought a journey to the city would be good for her health. It is known that Dickinson was anticipating her entry into Mount Holyoke that fall, and perhaps she was suffering anxiety over her performance on the entrance exams. On this trip, she did some sightseeing in and around Boston. She describes in her letter seeing Bunker Hill, climbing to the top of the state house, as well as attending two concerts and a horticultural exhibit. She also visited Mount Auburn Cemetery, the first landscaped garden cemetery in the United States. Compared to the small bare plots outside her window on West Street, the lush landscaping of Mount Auburn impressed Dickinson, who wrote to Abiah that it seemed as though nature itself had created the final resting place for those buried there.

If cemeteries and insane asylums strike twenty-first-century readers as odd places to visit on trips intended to lift one's spirits, it might be worth noting the times(the middle-nineteenth century) as well as the poet's family interests. The country was still young; the western states did not yet exist; settlement by Europeans was still expanding into Native American lands. Tourist attractions designed for pleasure trips were fewer and of a different nature than existed later (the National Park System, for example, would not come into being until 1872). In addition, over several generations, both the Dickinsons and the Norcrosses had a long tradition of active and personal interest in what was actively being built and promoted at the time—city and town institutions and infrastructure—including churches, railroads, college campuses and buildings, cemeteries, parks, and so forth. These kinds of places naturally struck them as worth noting and admiring when visiting other towns and cities. Edward's political career no doubt made such civic mindedness part of the conversation of many evening meals. On the other hand, it cannot be denied that asylums, cemeteries, and other sites also made their mark on Emily Dickinson's sensibilities as a poet, where nature, death, and emotional struggle are distinctly prominent themes.

City institutions aside, for the young poet still in her teens, the temporary Chinese Museum that was set up in Marlboro's Chapel was of such a curiosity that she writes an extended paragraph in the letter to Abiah dedicated to it alone. Speaking of the Chinese professor of music who was there with a Chinese writing teacher, she tells her friend that they were told the two were trying to kick their habit of eating opium at home in China by coming to the United States to live and work. Interestingly, she describes admiring their "self denial." She writes Abiah that for twelve and one-half cents the Chinese writing teacher gave out cards with the names of the visitors written on them in Chinese. Emily and Vinnie both got one, Emily relates, and confided that she considered the card one of her prized possessions. Readers looking for Asian influences on the poet's writing might consider this brief visit as one early source.

Another prominent site Dickinson relates seeing on this trip was the Bunker Hill Monument in Charlestown, then having been in place for just over 20 years. The monument was built as a tribute to the Revolutionary War's Battle of Bunker Hill. The obelisk itself was heralded as a feat of American technology when it was erected in 1825 to celebrate the 50th anniversary of the 1775 battle. Standing 221 feet high, the monument took 18 years to build. The construction required quarrying 6,600 tons of granite in Quincy, Massachusetts, and then transporting it first by horse-drawn carts, then by barge down the Neponset River, and later by a railroad that was built for the purpose of bringing the stone to the site. Climbing the 294 steps inside to the top allowed a view of the city and the Charles River. Whether she made the climb and looked out over the city, contemplating her future in a few weeks' time at college, one can only guess. The poet merely lists the monument in her letter as one of the sites she saw. Immediately after mentioning the monument, she goes back to discuss Mount Auburn Cemetery, which apparently made more of an impression on her. In her letter she imagines how the dead may feel being buried in such lovely, park-like surroundings.

One striking sentence in the letter to Abiah from the 1846 trip to Boston is that Dickinson describes herself visiting her aunt's family and feeling "happy," then retracts that word and substitutes the word "content." It is one of the few times we see her say so unabashedly that she is happy, and it is additional support for the difference in emotional atmospheres between the Dickinson and Norcross households. It also speaks to Dickinson's loyalty to her own family that she seems to indicate that she could not, or perhaps should not, be so well as to be happy in a home other than her own.

In 1851, when she was 20, the poet visited her relatives in Worcester and Boston again, this time for about two weeks with Vinnie. By now, Emily had already left Mount Holyoke and returned home to West Street where she had enjoyed the company of Austin's circle of friends before he went to Boston to teach for a short time. She and Vinnie met up with him there on this trip. Besides visiting the cemetery on Grove Street in Worcester (probably to pay tribute to Uncle William Dickinson's wife, Eliza Howley Dickinson, who had just died and had been buried there the month before), notable aspects of this trip included seeing the newly opened Boston Museum. The museum, which was advertised as having several museums in one, was where Vinnie reports in her diary that they saw Shakespeare's *Othello* performed. Another treat was having ice cream at an ice cream saloon,—a kind of place that would later be called an ice cream parlor. Ice cream was only then beginning to be mass produced at a cheaper cost than homemade ice cream. This change in production resulted from improved freezers and, in particular, the railroad's ability to transport milk and ice quickly to manufacturers. The ice cream saloon was new in Boston, and Emily and Vinnie apparently enjoyed it, because Vinnie records in her diary that they went there three times during the hot September of their 1851 visit.

They witnessed the Railroad Jubilee, which celebrated the six railroads and eight terminals in Boston, and featured a procession including President Fillmore (an event that had to come back in Emily's memory two years later when she witnessed her own father's triumph in bringing the Amherst-Belchertown branch line to town). They visited the Boston Custom House, lauded by Walt Whitman for its fine architecture even as Nathaniel Hawthorne continued to work at the old one nearby. While in the bigger city, Emily and Vinnie also apparently sought medical advice for ailments they'd had recently at home and received some prescriptions that Emily indicated later eased her symptoms.

Austin was teaching mostly Irish immigrant boys at the Endicott School in Boston, and the sisters visited him there during their stay. Making the trip across the ocean following turbulent days during the potato famine to arrive in a land where their parents had to work especially long and hard hours to make a go of it, the boys in Austin's charge were likely a handful at times for the privileged son of a small-town lawyer. Emily couldn't wait to see Austin, whom she had missed so much since he left Amherst. Seeing his new surroundings was probably the highlight of the trip for her. Friends Eliza Coleman and Abby Wood were in Boston for the Railroad Jubilee, and the three Dickinson siblings, now 22, 20, and 18, visited them. Strange as it may seem to admirers of the poet today, Vinnie records that the sisters also did some shopping.

Other than having the opportunity to see Austin, perhaps the most profound effect of this trip on the poet came from the fact that she was now in her early adulthood and had seen the city several times. It was the beginning of the awkward period for her when her friends were beginning to acquire, or move into, teaching positions or were otherwise acting on plans for their futures. Yet she was returning to the house on West Street with apparently no future plans, at least plans in the conventional sense. Perhaps this trip signaled in her a moment to make a decision of some similar kind, an adult choice that began to express her future adult identity. Something about the city on this trip did not appeal to her. Perhaps it was the fast pace of their activities in a short, two-week period; perhaps it was the crowds brought to town by the Railroad Jubilee, or something else altogether. Certainly, she wanted to dissuade Austin from staying in Boston much longer because she missed him so terribly; she wanted him to return to Amherst and perhaps feared he would be too lured by the hustle and bustle of the big city. Perhaps Austin's working conditions frustrated and tainted the view of the city he shared with his sisters. In any case, beginning with her return from this trip, Dickinson seems to have made a conscious choice of a preference for country life. While she would visit cities again in the future (Washington, D.C. and Philadelphia just four years later), she seems to have made a decision after this trip that none of them could ever be considered home. She would go home and begin the arduous task of finding her occupation at home as an artist. She did not return to the Boston area for 13 years. Ironically, those trips turned out to be her longest stays away from home yet.

CAMBRIDGE

From April 1864 to November of that year, and again from April 1, 1865, until the following October, the poet lived in Cambridge, Massachusetts, where she went for eye treatments with Dr. Henry W. Williams, a physician and oculist. Most readers are unaware of, and even many Dickinson scholars often forget, this long spell the poet spent away from Amherst, living about 13 months out of a two-year period in the city. She stayed with her Norcross cousins, Fanny and Loo (Frances and Louisa) in a boarding house at 86 Austin Street, Cambridgeport. The boarding house was owned by bookkeeper Barnabas Bangs, who lived there with his family. Louise and Frances Norcross, ages 21 and 16 respectively, were now orphaned; Emily's dear Aunt Lavinia and Uncle Loring had both passed away. They seem to have welcomed their cousin Emily, then 34, as one would perhaps a younger sister of their mother's rather than as the older cousin that she actually was.

A mother-child relationship developed with Emily adopting Fanny and Loo as her "children" in her letters when she was apart from them. She wrote many of her most intimate and open letters to the Norcross cousins, as the two have come to be called. However, the copies that currently exist were transcribed by them after Emily's death. Sentences and sections they did not want shared with the world were not recorded. The cousins, apparently out of a fierce desire to protect the genius mother-figure they loved so dearly, destroyed the originals of her letters to them.

With her eyes needing treatment, Dr. Williams advised the poet not to strain them by writing, so not many of her letters survive from the time she spent in Cambridge. Those that do express comfort in the care of her young cousins' and Mrs. Bangs's attentions to her needs, but a sadness at living in what she termed a "prison." This could refer to her small living quarters, necessarily kept dark for her eyes, within the confines of a small house with little or no yard on a busy street in a noisy city. Compared to the openness of her upstairs bedroom at the Homestead, overlooking Main Street and The Evergreens, with her garden and grounds and her dog and her conservatory of plants, the poet's long months in Cambridge were only spared by two saving graces. One was the affection of her dear young cousins and the other was the small amount of writing it appears she did accomplish while there, using the darker medium of pencil that was easier to see than pen. Arriving in early spring and leaving in the fall of each of the two years, the poet spent two entire summers there, with months stretching at either end, so that she experienced the rise in the city's temperatures, the full congestion of heat and humidity at its peak in midsummer, and the coolness of the fall evenings before she could head home to her beloved Amherst once again.

Shortly after her arrival for her second bout of eye treatments, events in the nation must have made living in Boston a time of even more heightened excitement and confusion. The Civil War ended with General Lee's surrender at Appomattox Courthouse, Virginia, on April 9, 1865, a week after she arrived in Cambridge. Then, Abraham Lincoln was assassinated at Ford's Theater in Washington, D.C. a few days later. In one letter to Vinnie, the poet mentions Jefferson Davis's capture on May 10. The day-to-day news of the surrender and its early aftermath were a part of the fabric of everyday life across the country, but this would have been magnified more so in an important historical city such as Boston.

It is interesting to consider that Emily Dickinson, who had spent her life in the small town of Amherst as her parents' caretaker and a poet, and who had just spent the previous three years writing at the most furious pace she would ever work composing what would be the largest share of her poems, was now at risk of losing her sight and living extended periods in a bustling city at one of the most critical times in the nation's history. Her letters indicate she found Cambridge, either due to her treatments or city life or both, suffocating. She once said in a letter that she couldn't sentence Carlo to "jail" by bringing him with her. It is clear from her letters home that she missed her family in Amherst very much.

The poet described her long months of eye treatments as painful. Scholars have pieced together a diagnosis that Dickinson's eye ailment was quite possibly anterior uveitas, or rheumatic iritis. The disease is characterized by aching eyes that grow more painful in the evenings, even after attempting to rest them during the day. Light aggravates the discomfort. The ailment must have been terrifying for the poet, who depended so heavily on her eyes for reading and writing. Even getting to Dr. Williams's home office, a new brownstone home located on the site now occupied by the Ritz-Carlton Hotel, may have been unpleasant for her. Each appointment would have meant riding in a carriage through all the noise produced by the soap factories, printing shops, and other industries springing up in that part of the city, the stores, offices, street vendors, immigrants, heat, and commotion.

On the other hand, Fanny and Loo shared their books and warm talks that likely involved the exchanging of secrets and young women's dreams and desires. They likely read Shakespeare aloud to the poet to rest her eyes, since later both cousins showed an interest in the stage. Apparently, one visitor, Charlotte Sewall Eastman, inscribed her gift of *Jane Eyre* to the poet, September 20, 1865. Asa and Lucretia Dickinson Bullard still lived nearby, as did Uncle Joel Norcross. The cousins' friends, as well as Mrs. Bangs, Dr. Williams, visitors from home and elsewhere when they were in the city, took care of her and kept her company. These, and books as she was allowed and letters as she could afford the eyesight to write and read, and her poetry—her "guests" in prison as she called her poems of this period—all these must have served as sustenance to her.

Very little else is known about Dickinson's life and times in the city. The Norcross cousins could certainly have shed light on this had they cared to do so, but they preferred to respect the poet's privacy and keep their personal memories of those days to themselves. What we do know is that apparently the poet's eyes did respond to Dr. Williams's prolonged treatments. In October 1865 she rode the train out of the city through the glorious New England fall foliage toward Amherst. When she stepped over the threshold of her father's house on Main Street Emily Dickinson was back home for good. At 34, she was never known to leave Amherst again.

NOTES

1. See Georgiana Strickland, "Emily Dickinson's Colorado," *Emily Dickinson Journal* 8 no. 1 (1999): pp. 1–23.

2. Dickinson letter to Mrs. J. G. Holland, March 18, 1855 (Dickinson, *Letters*, Johnson, ed., 3 vol.).

3. Qtd. in Habegger, *"Wars,"* p. 176.

4. Dickinson letter to Abiah Root, September 8, 1846 (Dickinson, *Letters*, Johnson, ed., 3 vol.).

Chapter 6

A POET'S READING

Like all artists, a poet is influenced by her family, friends, milieu, and the events that happen in her life and in her times; Emily Dickinson is no exception. Looking at all of these factors without considering another large influence—the poet's reading—would be to ignore one of the most profound and direct impacts upon her work. As might be expected, despite her father's early guidance of her reading toward the Bible and inspirational works, with the help of Austin and Susan, Dickinson managed to cultivate her own reading interests. The Dickinson family library that was removed from the Homestead shows few books bearing the poet's name, which would indicate her ownership of them. Her father had a penchant for not wanting her to read popular books, but then would look the other way when they mysteriously appeared in the house. Perhaps this explains why so many of them bear the inscription, bookplate, or other sign of ownership from other family members. A great many of the books from the Homestead bore Susan Dickinson's signature, which shows the generous extent to which she shared her collection with her "sister" across the lawn.

Possibly among the earliest readings the poet encountered were the children's and evangelical monthlies to which Edward subscribed for her and Austin. These included *Parley's Magazine*, an entertainment magazine for children that included monthly sections on travel, biography, history, poetry, moral tales, and puzzles. The magazine was published by Samuel Goodrich from 1833 to 1844. In the year Edward first subscribed, 1838, this article appeared: "Gleanings and Recollections: The New York Fire," by Eliza Leslie, which describes the New York City fire of 1835 when five hundred to seven hundred businesses were lost and firefighting efforts were hampered by the winter cold. A poem in *Parley's* that year included "A Visit from St. Nicholas" by Clement Moore (already popular); but in the January 1839 issue appeared a sentimental and morbid verse, "The Dying Boy," by "Mrs. Larned of Providence," taken from the apparently true story of an entire family of a mother and three children dying off from the husband and father's alcoholic neglect. In the poem the mother dies in childbirth, followed by the boy's sister, whose death grip still holds the boy's arm. In the verse, the boy searches his mother's blank stare, uncomprehendingly, "Can't I be dead too, mother, say? / I'm sure 'tis very lonesome here—"[1] Readers of Dickinson's poetry about death may recognize early influences in this reading.

In 1837, Edward subscribed to the *Sabbath School Visiter*, edited by Asa Bullard, the poet's uncle by marriage. Its stories were even less cheerful than some of those in *Parley's*. Samples from the year the Dickinsons subscribed—and likely the poet was sitting next to Austin reading together—include several horrifying stories of child martyrs meeting dreadful deaths but professing Christianity at just the right moment: "Charles's Last Sickness," "An Infant Missionary's Dying Gift," and "The Lost Finger" are just a few of these sensational and gory tales. The Bible and early hymnals such as those by Isaac Watts also contributed to the poet's early indoctrination with Christianity, language, and verse. Clearly, death, child personae, and immortality were themes and devices the poet came to know early on in her reading that would resurface later in her writing.

Dickinson's textbooks at Amherst Academy and Mount Holyoke had a profound effect on her. After so much frightening fire-and-brimstone reading at home, science books that attempted to explain the workings of the world in a straightforward, nonfrightening manner perhaps greatly appealed to her. Her textbooks at Amherst Academy and Mount Holyoke included, among others, *Elementary Geology* by Edward Hitchcock, *Elements of Mental Philosophy* by Thomas Cogswell Upham, *Familiar Lectures on Botany* by Almira Hart Lincoln Phelps, and *Manual of Botany, for North America* by Amos Eaton. Readers of Dickinson's poems cannot miss the references to flowers, gems, volcanoes, hills, and other natural wonders that reflect her coursework in these areas. Her early school copy of *Murray's Grammar* poses this interesting lesson about the use of the dash for which Dickinson would become so well-known for using in her poetry years later:

Of the Dash.

The Dash, though often used improperly by hasty and incoherent writers, may be introduced with propriety, where the sentence breaks off abruptly; where a significant pause is required; or where there is an unexpected turn in the sentiment...[2]

Readers of Dickinson's poetry recognize that her familiarity and reliance on the dash breaks this rule repeatedly and artfully.

Dickinson wrote in a letter to Thomas W. Higginson that for several years her lexicon was her only companion. The poet's dictionary was an 1844 reprint of the 1841 edition of Noah Webster's *An American Dictionary of the English Language* (interestingly, Webster was another Amherst native). Based on Webster's first American dictionary published in 1828 and for which many of the entries are the same, Dickinson's edition was also based on entries that used the Bible in definitions as examples.

The book that Austin smuggled into the Homestead past Mr. and Mrs. Dickinson and hid under the piano cover for Emily to read was *Kavanagh* by Henry Wadsworth Longfellow. The book appeared in 1849, and that is the date of Austin's copy in the family library. *Kavanagh* is a romantic novel about small-town life and literary ambition, making it certainly worth closer study for the way it may have affected Dickinson's sensibilities as she entered early adulthood. Markings in the copy suggest that she, Susan, Austin, and perhaps other friends pored over it either together or consecutively, highlighting passages that reminded them of themselves, each other, or issues of their concerns or conversations.

Another book from around the same time that seemed to provide a subject of much discussion and debate among this same circle was *Reveries of a Bachelor,* by Ik Marvel, pseudonym of Donald Mitchell. In *Reveries*, a bachelor stares into the fire one evening and imagines the entire scenario of a married life in great detail, to the point that he can convince himself such a life is not for him. This conclusion is questioned in the latter part of the novel. Dickinson refers to this book often in her letters to Susan in the early 1850s. Clearly, she, Susan, and Austin, were exploring their futures as young adults interested in literature in a world that encouraged marrying, settling down, and raising a family. The struggle between the individual artist's life and domestic duties and other expectations of society would be a subject of many of Dickinson's poems.

It is primarily through books and writing that the poet and Susan Gilbert appeared to have come together. Since they both thought of themselves as *poets* and all others as *prose,* they separated themselves from the rest of their friends as special, more committed, more artful in their writing. Emerson's famed essay, "Thoughts on Modern Literature" must have been in the young writer's minds:

Goethe, then must be set down as the poet of the Actual, not of the Ideal; the poet of limitation, not of possibility; of this world, and not of religion and hope; in short, if I may say so, the poet of prose, and not of poetry.[3]

Decidedly, not many years after her nineteen-year-old musings with Susan about reveries, poets, and prose, Dickinson would take Emerson's challenge and become a poet of possibility: "I dwell in Possibility - / A fairer House than Prose - ".

Dickinson read the *Springfield Republican* daily and kept up with several other periodicals such as *Scribner's*, *The Atlantic Monthly*, and *Harper's*. From these publications she would have gleaned not only information about current events nationally but also locally. The newspapers of those days announced when an individual in Amherst bought a new horse, or when a visitor had come to stay with an Amherst family. In the magazines the poet would have read essays, short stories, and poetry by some of the best American writers publishing in her day. These periodicals are worth a deeper look by more scholars when examining literary influences on the poet. When she writes that she never read Walt Whitman's *Leaves of Grass*, for example, having heard, perhaps from Dr. Holland's review in the *Republican* that he was "disgraceful," she may have read individual poems of Whitman's published in periodicals.

Perhaps one of the last devotionals the poet read as an adult was *Of the Imitation of Christ*, which preached the value of daily rituals and a monastic life. It appears that Susan gave her a copy of this book, but the reason why she did so is unclear. Some scholars see a connection in what might be called Dickinson's renunciation of conventional life to devote her living to writing poetry as stemming from ideas she read here.

When Thomas Wentworth Higginson asked the poet what she read, she responded in an 1862 letter that she read poets John Keats (her poem, "I died for Beauty" echoes his "Death on a Grecian urn"), and Robert Browning and Elizabeth Barrett Browning. She was particularly taken with the latter Browning's *Aurora Leigh*. For prose, she mentioned essayists John Ruskin and Sir Thomas Browne, a seventeenth-century British physician and author who attempted to reconcile science and religion. She also mentioned the Book of Revelation in the Bible. While she mentions the Brownings several times later on in life, this letter is one of the few times she mentions Ruskin and Keats; it is possible she did so because Higginson cites them in his article.

Her adult reading preferences would also come to include Shakespeare's plays, Charles Dickens's novels, Charlotte Brontë's *Jane Eyre, Vil-*

lette, and others, and Emily Brontë's poems. She read Nathaniel Hawthorne's *The House of the Seven Gables* the year it came out, commenting about Hepzibah and Clifford's sibling relationship in a letter to Austin. She also read Thoreau's *Walden*, and several volumes of Emerson's poems and essays appear in the library, including *The Conduct of Life* (1861, 1879), *Society and Solitude* (1879), *May-Day* (1867), and *Essays* (1861). She once labeled Emerson's *Representative Men* in a letter as a book of "granite" that could be leaned upon.[4]

Dickinson's reading affected her work in several ways, including providing subject matter, technique, allusion, and, perhaps most importantly, examples of successful writing by women such as the Brontë sisters, Elizabeth Barrett Browning, and George Eliot. While some work has begun in Dickinson scholarship to look for direct influences between authors and works in Dickinson's poems, much more work needs to be done in this rich area.

NOTES

1. *Parley's Magazine*, January, 1839, pp. 12–13; reprinted from the *Christian Keepsake*.

2. Murray, *An English Grammar*, p. 278.

3. Emerson, *Prose and Poetry*, p. 346.

4. Dickinson letter to Mary Higginson, Christmas, 1876 (Dickinson, *Letters*, Johnson, ed., 3 vols.).

*Emily Norcross Dickinson,
the poet's mother, probably
taken at the same sitting as
the poet's daguerreotype,
c. 1846–1847. Mrs. Dickinson was well educated and
passed on her love of home
and nature to her daughter.
Photo courtesy of Monson
Free Library and Reading
Room Association. Photo-
graphic copy by Henry
Peach.*

*Edward Dickinson, the poet's
father, in 1853. About him the
poet wrote, "His Heart was
pure and terrible." In 1851, he
rang the church bell so that the
townspeople would not miss
seeing the aurora borealis in the
night skies over Amherst.
Photo by permission of The
Houghton Library, Harvard
University. MS Am 1118.99b
(16) © The President and
Fellows of Harvard College.*

William Austin Dickinson commencement picture from Amherst College, 1850. As young people, the poet and her brother shared books, jokes, and a circle of friends. Austin followed his father's footsteps as an attorney and treasurer of Amherst College. Amherst College Archives, Amherst, Ma.

Lavinia Norcross Dickinson, the poet's sister, in the 1850s. Vinnie protected Emily during her lifetime but after the poet died, she wanted her poems read "everywhere." Emily called her a "Soldier and Angel." Todd-Bingham Picture Collection, Manuscripts and Archives Yale University Library.

Susan Huntington Gilbert Dickinson, the poet's sister-in-law. Emily wrote more letters and poems to her sister-in-law than to anyone else. In one letter she wrote, "we are the only poets, and everyone else is prose." Several of her letters to Susan had sections crossed out, erased, or scissored away after her death. Photo by permission of The Houghton Library, Harvard University. MS Am 1118.99b (29.4) © The President and Fellows of Harvard College.

The Dickinson Homestead on Main Street, Amherst, Massachusetts, 1886. Emily was born and died here, though she also lived on Pleasant Street (then West St.) for several years in her youth. The poet's two bedroom windows facing the street are visible behind the trees at the far left of the second story. Photo by permission of The Houghton Library, Harvard University. MS Am 1118.99b (79) © The President and Fellows of Harvard College.

The Evergreens, c. 1870. Built in 1856 next door to the Homestead by Edward Dickinson for his son and daughter-in-law, the Italianate villa became a center for social gatherings in Amherst as well as a lively family home where the poet's niece and nephews played as children. By permission of the Jones Library, Inc., Amherst, Massachusetts.

Emily Dickinson's bedroom at the Homestead where she did most of her writing. From her corner windows the poet could observe "Society" to the south on Main Street and loved ones to the west at the Evergreens. Photo by Frank Ward. Courtesy of the Emily Dickinson Museum.

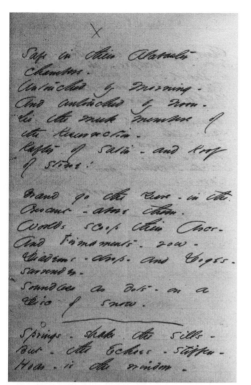

A fair copy of the poem "Safe in their Alabaster Chambers" in the poet's hand. The first stanza of "Springs - shake the sills - " appears at the bottom of the page. In her writing portfolio, the poet often drew horizontal lines between poems. This page is from a sewn packet later labeled by editors Fascicle 10. Photo by permission of The Houghton Library, Harvard University. MS Am 1118.3 (203) © The President and Fellows of Harvard College.

Emily Dickinson's gravestone at West Cemetery in Amherst. Flowers and other tributes are still left at the gravesite by those who continue to be moved by the poet's words. By permission of Connie Ann Kirk.

Chapter 7

THE "FLOOD" YEARS AND THE CIVIL WAR

When most students read an Emily Dickinson poem or discuss the mysteries of her life, most are looking at the period from 1861 to 1865, or what editor Thomas H. Johnson called the "flood" years of Dickinson's poetic production. During these years, the poet wrote approximately half of all of the nearly 1,800 poems that still exist. Some of her best-known and most powerful poetry was written in this period, including such poems as: "Some keep the Sabbath going to church - "; "Wild nights - Wild nights!"; "I'm ceded - I've stopped"; "A Bird, came down the / walk - "; "The Soul selects her own Society - "; "I died for Beauty, but"; "This was a Poet - "; "I dwell in Possibility - "; "Because I could not / stop for Death - "; "This is my letter to the world"; "I heard a Fly buzz - when / I died - "; "I started early - took my / Dog - "; "I cannot live with you - "; "The Props assist the House - "; "A Thought went up my mind / today - "; "A narrow Fellow in / the grass" and so many others. In 1862 alone the poet wrote an average of one finished poem per day.

There are different theories as to why this period was so prolific for her. The most frequently advanced theory states that she experienced a failed or forbidden love affair, which drove her to write some of her most impassioned and effective poems. Candidates suggested as the focus of her affections include Judge Otis P. Lord, Charles Wadsworth, and Samuel Bowles, among others.

Judge Lord was a friend and colleague of her father's who was appointed to the Massachusetts Superior Court in 1859. He visited the Homestead with his wife on June 9, 1860, and also delivered the Amherst College commencement address on July 9, 1862. The poet wrote to him, and they had an active exchange of letters after Lord's wife died several years after this period.

Charles Wadsworth was a minister and well-known speaker at the Arch Street Presbyterian Church in Philadelphia. It is believed Emily heard him speak at the church in 1855 when she visited Philadelphia with her sister after the trip to Washington, D.C. when her father was a congressman. She and Wadsworth corresponded afterward, and she reportedly sought his counsel. Wadsworth was also a married man. He did come to call on Emily in Amherst during the spring of 1860. He and his family set sail for San Francisco on May 1, 1862.

Samuel Bowles was an editor of the *Springfield Republican* and was a frequent guest of his good friends Austin and Susan Dickinson at The Evergreens. Emily was known to enjoy late nights there with her brother and sister-in-law's company, especially in the early years of their marriage. Bowles was part of these occasions as were other friends such as Kate Scott Anchon and Maria Whitney. Bowles was a raucous, forthright man who liked to tease, and Emily corresponded with him and sent him several poems. Because he was such a good friend of Austin and Susan's, he was a fairly regular part of their lives. He published one of Dickinson's poems anonymously in the *Springfield Republican*, reportedly without her approval. That was "I taste a liquor never brewed - " which he printed under the title "The May Wine." In May 1861, Bowles published "Safe in their Alabaster Chambers" under the title, "The Sleeping." He sailed for Europe in April of 1862. That same month Dickinson wrote to Thomas Wentworth Higginson, editor at *The Atlantic Monthly*, sending him four poems and asking for his comments on them.

Though each of these three men was married, did not live in Amherst, had entered Dickinson's life and correspondence, then left her for some period in the early 1860s, there is still a problem with attempting to identify any of them as the inspiration of Dickinson's passionate poems. There are arguments that can be presented in favor of each of them and arguments that can be made against each of them. There is, so far, no definitive documentary evidence that pins down anyone in particular as the poet's love interest during the 1860s. Readers and scholars have tried for over 100 years to identify Emily's muse, but no one knows for sure if that person was Lord, Wadsworth, Bowles, Susan Dickinson, someone else, or no one in particular. Good and intriguing arguments have been made for each of them. It could very well be that some combination of people in her life, their company and correspondence followed by her feeling their slipping away by degrees prompted her to write poems. It could also be imagination or some other sense of loss that precipitated the depth of poetry she produced.

Besides forbidden or failed love affairs or relationships, there may have been other reasons for the poet's productivity in the early to mid-1860s. Edward (Ned) Dickinson, Austin and Susan's first child, was born June 19, 1861. Having a child changes the dynamics of a family, especially a first child for a couple who has been used to frequently entertaining out-of-town guests and hosting late night parties. Recall that Austin and Susan had been married and living at The Evergreens since 1856 and were entertaining guests as prestigious as Ralph Waldo Emerson by 1857. They were married nearly five years by the time Ned was born; there had been plenty of time to get used to a house with no children (though, actually, young family members such as orphaned Clara and Anna Newman, daughters of Edward's sister, Mary, did occasionally stay at The Evergreens for extended periods). For her part, though, there is much evidence that Emily loved children. There are suggestions that she may have been a bit uneasy around babies, especially newborns. When Ned was born, for example, Emily sent Susan a poem across the lawn in which the speaker says she would have come herself but she feared "joggling" the baby.[1] Though she often wrote to new mothers to congratulate them on the joyous occasion of the births of their babies, there is no documented evidence of Dickinson holding or playing with an infant.

It is possible that the change over at The Evergreens with the birth of Ned had a strong impact on her. At the same time Susan first became a mother, Emily was solidifying her vocation as a poet and moving into a heightened state of poetic production and refinement. Perhaps Ned's birth inspired her to create just as it inspired Susan to accept the new responsibilities and joys of motherhood. Perhaps, as some suggest, Susan's attentions away from Emily as a result of Ned's birth drove the poet to turn more toward her poems. The suggestion that she was jealous of the boy is likely too strong; it is more likely that the two women enjoyed the different changes happening in both of their lives at the time. Perhaps Susan's attentions to the new baby in some way removed a distraction or provided an incentive that drove Emily to write even more.

Aside from love affairs and the birth of her first nephew, another theory that has developed over the years as to why Dickinson may have been writing so much and so furiously during this period is that she may have been suffering from an emotional or mental disturbance, for which she sought out her poetry as a means of therapy. She writes to Thomas Wentworth Higginson in April of 1862 that she suffered a "terror" since the previous September that she could tell to no one. Speculation abounds as to the causes and nature of this fright or emotional disturbance. Some scholars have argued that Dickinson may have been suffering from a nervous breakdown; others claim she was deep in depression. Recent analysis suggests severe anxiety, perhaps with a particularly virulent attack in the fall of 1861 for reasons left unexplained.

Whatever the reason or motivation or combination of factors, Dickinson wrote a range and depth and complexity of poetry in 1861–1865 that is simply startling to even the most critical of observers. The poems appear, one after another, seemingly with ease, yet increasingly fraught with indecision about variations in word choices and other matters that she notes in her increasing collection of portfolios. Many of the poems are masterpieces about nature, death, love, immortality, and other subjects. Dickinson had reached the height of her poetic powers in a frenzy of writing that seemed almost unstoppable. Though she wrote many poems before and after these years that readers still cherish today, had it not been for her work during this period, it is likely that we would never have heard of Emily Dickinson. When considered in terms of her full biography, however, the need for this time period to be placed in context becomes even more apparent—interestingly, these prolific years make up less than 10 percent of the poet's life span.

THOMAS WENTWORTH HIGGINSON

In April 1862, Thomas Wentworth Higginson, then an editor at *The Atlantic Monthly* to which the Dickinsons subscribed, published an article called "Letter to a Young Contributor" in the magazine. In this article, Higginson offers practical advice to young writers who would like to see their work in print. Among his many tips of advice were that the writer remember that every editor is human and to present his/her material in an attractive and readable manner; that the work be polished and require little editing; that writers "charge [their] style with life."[2] He also suggested that writers use neither too stiff nor too lax language; and that they take their time, among many other suggestions.

That Emily Dickinson was ready for some kind of professional response to her work, already years in the making, is evidenced in that she not only read the article, but she responded to it immediately. She wrote Higginson a letter on April 15, 1862. Instead of signing the letter, she enclosed her name in pencil on a card inside a smaller envelope. She enclosed four poems with the letter and directly asked for Higginson's impressions of them. In response to his call that writers' styles be charged with life, she wanted to know if he thought her verse were "alive." The poems she sent him then were: "Safe in their Alabaster Chambers," "The nearest Dream recedes unrealized," "We play at Paste," and "I'll tell you how the Sun rose."

It bears noting here that "Safe in their Alabaster Chambers," one of the poet's finest and best-known poems, is an important but single example yet to date of a previously little known fact about the poet's writing practice. It is commonly believed that the poet shut herself in her upstairs chamber and wrote without showing her poems to anyone until the time she mailed these few to Higginson. In fact, documents in the poet's own hand indicate that this early poem, dated by editor Ralph W. Franklin as around 1859, was sent across the lawn to The Evergreens for critique by Susan Dickinson, who at the time was childless and remained actively engaged in writing herself. Notes between the houses with comments on them show that the poet not only asked for Susan's advice on this poem but that she also actually changed the second verse at her sister-in-law's suggestion. This is the only known poem in Dickinson's entire corpus that is known to have been changed by the poet at the critique of another person. The change not only shows the comradery and confidence the poet shared with her sister-in-law at that time, but the correspondence about the poem also shows the poet wanting her brother and sister-in-law to be proud of her as a poet.[3] In the end, the poet did change the verse, taking Sue's suggestions into consideration but still keeping the poem very much her own. The poem was printed years later in the *Springfield Republican* in two stanzas under the title "The Sleeping." Another anonymous poem printed underneath it, "The Shadow of Thy Wing," may have been by Susan.

Higginson responded to the letter and four poems from the woman in Amherst right away. His letter does not survive, but the poet's second letter to him suggests what it may have contained. In her letter, dated April 25, 1862, she thanks him for his comments on her work, saying the "surgery" was not as painful as she thought it might be.[4] Apparently Higginson asked to know a little more about her because she relates information about her family, books she likes, and other matters. Importantly, she poses in this letter as a novice, saying that she had only begun writing verses the previous winter, when, in fact, the 31-year-old poet had been writing poetry for years by this time and was just coming into her prime in terms of depth of subject matter and mastery of technique. She enclosed three more poems with this letter which are believed to be: "There came a Day - at - / summer's full - ", "Of all the Sounds dispatched / abroad - ", and "South winds jostle them - ".

Apparently Higginson's next letter recommends that the poet delay an attempt to publish her work because in a statement in her third letter, out of truth or hurt pride or perhaps a mixture of both, the poet claims that publishing her poems was the furthest thing from her mind. Despite Higginson's failure to see Dickinson's potential and genius (her work was so unconventional for its time that he did not recognize its merit), the poet appreciated his correspondence and the opportunity to communicate with a professional editor about her work. Apparently, Higginson appreciated her clever turn of phrase and attempted to encourage her writing by keeping up their correspondence. Dickinson would go on to write Higginson over 70 letters—more letters than she would write to any other single correspondent except for her sister-in-law, Sue. Their epistolary relationship lasted 23 years. While Higginson is clearly one of the single most important figures in the poet's life and work, their relationship seems to be one of mentor to mentored (the poet asked Higginson to be her "preceptor") rather than a romantic one as was speculated upon in earlier studies. By initiating and writing approximately nine letters between 1862–1865, Dickinson's new relationship with Higginson meant a great deal to her as a writer and was an especially important one to her during this period when she took her poetry so seriously and was writing so much and so well.

Starting in 1865 and 1866, the white heat frenzy of poem making was beginning to subside, although Dickinson would continue to create beautiful poems and sew them into her booklets for many more years. More than one observer has noted that this time frame coincides roughly with both of her eye treatments that necessitated extended stays in Cambridge, Massachusetts, in 1864 and 1865, as well as with the death of her dog, Carlo, who had been her steady companion since 1850. After Carlo's death in January of 1866, the poet wrote to tell Higginson. In Carlo's absence, she asked who would teach her now? It is interesting how Dickinson seemed to connect teaching with solace and comfort and that her faithful Newfoundland was apparently her direct connection to nature as true companion and muse. By November 1866, Susan and Austin had another child, a daughter, Martha. For whatever reason, Emily started staying more and more at home and out of sight of acquaintances and others who came to the Homestead. The flood years of her creative output may have ceased, but the aftermath of their effect on her life and later work was yet to be determined.

DICKINSON AND THE CIVIL WAR

Most readers would not call Emily Dickinson a political poet. She did not go to the front lines, for example, like Louisa May Alcott, and treat the wounded, nor did she write elegies on the assassination of Abraham Lincoln like Walt Whitman. Neither, however, did she shut herself in her bedroom and ignore the war that was attempting to tear apart her country. That, and many other myths developed over the years that paint the poet as too isolated and sheltered to know much about, or to interact with, the outside world. A misconception developed that the poet not only did not write about the Civil War but that she was shielded from knowing very much about it.

Dickinson read the newspaper, and just as it is in the twenty-first century, war at that time was the source of constant news and conversation when it was happening. Day-to-day progress in the war was reported by journalists and generals; politicians expressed opinions; citizens on street corners argued about one action or policy or another; communities grieved for, and gave honor to, their dead soldiers whose bodies were returned home. Amherst, Massachusetts, was no exception during the Civil War, and the Dickinson household on Main Street, owned by a patriarch who had served in Congress only a few years earlier, must have heard and shared in the talk.

Although it may be argued that the main subjects of Dickinson's poetry are the exploration of one's interior life and space, consciousness, perception, eternity, and other issues that are perhaps more private than public, more personal than political, this does not mean that she did not write at all about the chaos of the war that was happening in her time and happened to coincide with her most prolific period. In one letter, for example, she writes of the death of an Amherst soldier, Frazar Stearns. Stearns was killed in action at the Battle of Newburn, North Carolina, in the Union victory there on March 14, 1862. Stearns's body may have been wheeled by her Homestead window in a funeral procession down Main Street. Dickinson was also aware of other local Civil War deaths, including the two Adams boys, sons of an Amherst College professor's widow. The poet, due to her father's and society's influence, may have seen politics as a topic for only men to discuss. However, it was the deaths war caused that moved the poet to write about it. Shira Wolosky argues in *Emily Dickinson: A Voice of War* that the martial imagery and themes in several poems of the 1861–1865 period reflect the poet's concern with the Civil War. In writing about death in battle, Dickinson's response to the war corresponds quite fittingly with American poets who would come after her.

While Edward Dickinson was clearly involved in the political scene leading up to the war in his stint in Congress in the mid-1850s, it must be noted that the Dickinsons were also guilty of bourgeois avoidance of getting too involved in the war. When a soldier who had apparently heard of Emily's conservatory plants stopped by to request of her a nosegay to carry with him for some purpose, she refused, writing about it later in seemingly indignant tones that he must have thought the Homestead was a place where flowers could be bought. When local Amherst women were weaving blankets and otherwise supporting the war effort through their domestic skills, Emily coldly refused to participate. When asked to submit a few lines with Susan for a publication intended to raise money to support the troops, both Emily and Susan refused. What is often read as uncaring in history to its readers may be seen as discomfort with, or a refusal to cooperate with, the war in general. However, one interprets it, this passive protest or arrogant avoidance of involvement, turns political and perhaps even more controversial when considering Austin's reaction to the draft. When he was drafted by the Union Army to serve in 1864, like others who could afford it then, Austin paid $500 for a poor Irishman to serve in his stead.

Even with these apparent withdrawals, scholar Karen Dandurand only recently discovered three Dickinson poems that were published in *Drum Beat,* a publication produced to support medical treatment of Union soldiers in Brooklyn. Unlike other poems published without the poet's consent in her lifetime, the poet, Dandurand argues, may have submitted these herself at the editor's request.[5] Thomas Wentworth Higginson broke off his frequent correspondence with the poet for a time when he was called up to lead the all-black Twenty-Ninth Regiment, the First South Carolina Volunteers, for the Union Army. Dickinson appeared to follow Higginson's experience through the war and wrote letters to him asking about his well-being. Somehow, he did manage to respond. Ironically, an uncle of Emily's, Edward's youngest brother, Samuel, had moved south to Georgia from Amherst years earlier to find his livelihood. That "Uncle Sam" Dickinson, Puritan roots and all, ended up fighting for the Confederate side against the Union; perhaps in some strange way this negated Austin's refusal to fight for the North. Matters of history are always more complicated than they seem at first glance.

Unlike what was first believed, scholars now mostly agree that there are several Dickinson poems, mostly dealing with death, that appear to be written in response to, or were inspired by, the Civil War. Among others, these include: "It feels a shame to be alive," "He fought like those who've nought to lose," "Wolfe demanded during dying," "It don't sound so terrible quite as it did," and "When I was small, a woman died." The poems explore issues of death, victory, and sacrifice. For Dickinson, the Civil War appeared to be a massive drama where these conflicts played out in serious consequence. If she was not involved as physically or publicly as a Whitman or an Alcott or other writers of the period, her imagination was certainly engaged by the horror of the war that took place in the country her family was so active in building at the local, state, and national levels. With her acute artistry she distills the war from the speeches, the causes, and the statistics and accountings of armies' victories and losses to the single, intimate moment of death of the individual soldier. By accomplishing that, Dickinson may have been thus far overlooked as a war poet. Though she was not a protest poet in the sense that twenty-first-century readers would most likely think of, her poems did succeed in making moments of war as vivid and personally engaging as any poet before her or after her has been able to do.

NOTES

1. Dickinson letter-poem to Susan Dickinson, c. June 19, 1861 (Dickinson, *Letters*, Johnson, ed., 3 vols.).

2. Thomas Wentworth Higginson, "Letter to a Young Contributor," *The Atlantic Monthly* 9 no. 54 (April 1862): p. 404.

3. "Emily Dickinson Writing a Poem," *Dickinson Electronic Archives*, available online: http://www.iath.virginia.edu/dickinson/safe/preintro.html.

4. Dickinson letter to Thomas W. Higginson, April 25, 1862 (Dickinson, *Letters*, Johnson, ed., 3 vols.).

5. Karen Dandurand, "New Dickinson Civil War Publications," *American Literature* 56 (March 1984): pp. 17–27.

Chapter 8

TO PRINT OR PUBLISH?

Emily Dickinson knew only 11 of her hundreds of poems to be published in print in her lifetime. Most of these were in newspapers; only one appeared in a book. "Success is counted sweetest" was published anonymously at Helen Fiske Hunt Jackson's special request in *The Masque of Poets*, published in 1878 by Roberts Brothers of Boston. The book was a collection of poems all published anonymously to encourage the guessing game of the poets' identities. "Success" was credited erroneously as being written by Ralph Waldo Emerson, a fact Jackson, if not Dickinson, found intriguing.

Some of Dickinson's poems were reprinted in other publications after their initial appearance. Most were published without her consent when poems sent to friends or family passed from them to editors without her knowledge or approval. Dickinson once said publication was like selling one's mind at auction and wrote to her preceptor Colonel Higginson, when he suggested that she wait to publish her very unconventional verse, that publication was the furthest thing from her mind.

Over the years, scholars have studied Dickinson's statements and practices in regard to publication to form a better understanding of what she may have thought about it. They point to Dickinson's initiation of her decades-long correspondence with Thomas Wentworth Higginson in April 1862 as an attempt to not only inquire of a professional editor whether her work had aesthetic literary value but also whether it was of publishable quality. Contrary to the "myth" of Amherst, who supposedly wrote alone in her room never sharing a line with family or friends and whose writing habit was unknown to anyone in the world until after her death, the poet Emily Dickinson copied poem after poem into letters and mailed them out herself in her own hand to family, friends, and acquaintances on a highly regular basis. Dickinson wrote well over 1,000 currently surviving letters and notes to at least 90 different correspondents in her lifetime. Correspondents number in the dozens who received the gift of her poems written originally or copied over especially for them in the form of verses or prose poetry as part of the letters. The number of poems sent as part of letters runs even higher. These dozens of people showed poems to others, some of whom were influential in the publishing world of the day. This hand circulation and word-of-mouth notoriety, as it were, made Emily Dickinson known as a poet during her lifetime, even among the literary community. Granted, her readers were of a smaller, more networked audience than commercially published poets of her time. Dickinson called this status of being a poet her "Barefoot-Rank."[1] This characterization brings to mind, perhaps, what people of the early twenty-first century might call a grass roots, alternative, or counterculture poet—an artist who is known to be authentic and true emerging to an appreciative, knowledgeable, though small, audience of her peers.

Dickinson's choice to avoid traditional publication should not strike twenty-first-century readers today as that unusual. Even now, poets in the United States make the same decision every day that Dickinson made. When their work is not deemed profitable for the big business of publishing conglomerates (for which poetry rarely is profitable), poets abandon traditional publishing and find other means of sharing their work. They may start presses of their own, pay for the production of a limited edition of chapbooks at their own expense, or as is done more recently, self-publish globally in the free, electronic medium of the Internet. In poetry, there is a long tradition of self-publishing in the United States, which extends back before Walt Whitman's first editions of *Leaves of Grass* forward to the twenty-first century with Internet hypertexts mounted on personal Web sites, or original poetry circulated around the world through email and listservs.

HELEN FISKE HUNT JACKSON

Editors such as Thomas Wentworth Higginson, Samuel Bowles, and Dr. Josiah Gilbert Holland all had copies of Dickinson poems in their possession at various times, but of these three only Bowles published any of them in the poet's lifetime. Interestingly, Dickinson was urged to "sing aloud" by Helen Fiske Hunt Jackson, an Amherst native and herself a well-known author at the time.[2]

The author of *Ramona, A Century of Dishonor,* and many other works not only repeatedly asked the poet to publish, but she also went so far as to ask to be named her literary executor, a request the poet summarily ignored. Knowing the family (Helen Fiske was delivered in 1830 by the same Dr. Cutler who would deliver the poet a few weeks later; and Helen had been a girlhood friend of Vinnie's), Jackson continued to press the poet, exchanging letters and poems. She even visited her at the Homestead. Fiske's fascination may have led, as some claim, to her modeling Esther Wynn in "Ester Wynn's Love-Letters," a short story in her collection, *Saxe Holm's Stories,* after the poet. Other scholars dispute this claim.

Her success in seeing "Success is counted sweetest," which she told the poet she knew by heart, published in *Masque of Poets,* must have come as small reward for Jackson's early recognition of the poet's talent. Perhaps if she had been allowed to edit the poems (she died a few months before Dickinson) their firm stature in world literature would have been established much earlier than it was. As it is, Dickinson's place is probably higher and more enduring in world literature than Jackson's.

Dickinson maintained an active audience and readership for her poetry by hand circulating her poems through personal letters. Perhaps this practice explains her refusal to publish when the opportunities to do so came to her later such as from supportive and influential Helen Hunt Jackson. Martha Nell Smith, in *Rowing in Eden: Rereading Emily Dickinson,* proposes an answer when she suggests that Dickinson thought very differently about the words *publish* and *print*.[3] She points to Dickinson's correspondence both with Higginson and with her sister-in-law, Sue, her two most frequent correspondents, as distinguishing *print* as the mechanical setting of manuscript words into typeface reprinted over and over by presses and *publishing* as the dissemination of poems to an audience by a variety of means, including hand-to-hand circulation of handwritten originals and copies.

The few poems Dickinson did see emerge in print suffered from editorial alterations the likes of which she did not approve. For example, Dickinson did not title most of her poems. At least one reason must be that the words of a title would take up, in some cases, over 10 percent of the entire poem since most of the poems are very short. When "A narrow Fellow in / the grass" appeared in the *Springfield Republican* under the title imposed by the editor "The Snake," the entire effect of the riddle poem, which is a revelation to the reader of what the narrow fellow is, was taken away, or as Dickinson says, and Smith reminds us, the poem was "defeated"[4] when it appeared in print. Dickinson's letters indicate her recognition and dis-

approval of such seemingly minor alterations as differences in punctuation. In the art of poetry, a comma or question mark or dash is as important as the stroke of the artist's brush in achieving an overall desired
effect. Changing such a minor detail can damage the poem as much as
cutting a chunk out of a work of sculpture, or changing the colors of the
sky in one corner of the canvas of an oil painting. The hand of the editor
on Dickinson's poems in her lifetime was heavy, indeed.

Aesthetically speaking, critics such as Susan Howe, Marta Werner, and
others press the issue of poetry's publication in print even further. They
point to the aesthetic value of the handwritten manuscript itself as an
artistic artifact. The handwriting, its position on the page, the kind and
orientation of the paper with the pencil lead or ink upon it, stray markings, doodles, or sketches, line breaks in relation to the shape of the paper
used, and other distinctions. All of these factors together, they argue, contribute to the overall effect of the handwritten poetic manuscript and the
experience encountering it has on an audience. Even today, print technology may be regarded as ill equipped and as one dimensional when used
to reproduce poetry as it is when reproducing the three-dimensional art
form of sculpture or the textural qualities of original paintings.

Whether Dickinson appears to have thought through the presentation
of her poems to the degree of their visual quality on the page or not (her
preparation of the portfolios lends some support to the argument that she
may have cared about this), she was definitely let down in two ways by the
traditional publishing community of her day. First, through its failure to
recognize the genius of her work in its unconventionality when she first
offered it for professional review; and secondly by homogenizing her work
or otherwise damaging it through poor editing when it did make a rare appearance in print. Add to this Dickinson's penchant for constant revision
in her writing practice. Not only did she change poems before she sent
them to various correspondents, but she also continually edited them in
her portfolios. Most writers must learn to live with changes they would
like to make in their work after they see it go to print. Perhaps keeping the
possibilities open by not confining the words to print was important to
her. Sharon Cameron argues in *Choosing Not Choosing: Dickinson's Fascicles* that the poet had trouble making final word choices in her manuscript
books and ultimately left the choices and final decisions open to the
reader. These reasons, either separately or combined, establish reasonable
rationale for why Dickinson did not publish more often in traditional
print in her lifetime.

Instead, the struggle of that endeavor, with its inevitable choices, judg-
ments, difficulties, and concerns, fell upon editors, who could not bear to

see this work destroyed or suppressed, to contend with the problem of editing it after her death. Pushing ahead without the author's cooperation, editing her work became a messy and imprecise affair, an ordeal that continues to this day with unanswerable questions. As we shall see, some editors have been more successful than others at the monumental task of preparing nearly 1,800 poems for print. Were it not for their decisions and painstaking work, however, we may have never known the pleasure of Dickinson's poetry and letters—however problematic the texts of them continue to be.

NOTES

1. Dickinson letter to Thomas W. Higginson, June 7, 1862 (Dickinson, *Letters*, Johnson, ed., 3 vols.).

2. Jackson letter to the poet, late 1876 (Dickinson, *Letters*, Johnson, ed., 3 vols.).

3. Smith, *Rowing*, p. 11.

4. Qtd. in Smith, *Rowing*, p. 11.

Chapter 9

LATER YEARS, LAST DAYS

CARLO

Odd as it may seem to a first-time reader of Dickinson's biography, but a sad event around January 1866 conveniently separates this later period in the poet's life from what went on before, and that was the death of the poet's Newfoundland, Carlo, her constant companion for over 15 years. The dog had been given to her by her father when they still lived at the West Street house; the poet was 19 and home for good from Mount Holyoke. Carlo apparently relieved the poet of the uneasiness she may have experienced when going out alone. At least one firsthand account describes Carlo lying by the poet's side as she played the piano at The Evergreens at one of the late-night gatherings in which she took part in the early days of Austin and Susan's marriage. Several other accounts around town document Carlo's accompanying the poet everywhere she went. Carlo made the walk with her and the family to the Homestead from the West Street house in 1855. It is likely that Carlo could be seen alongside her as she worked in the garden and that he was allowed inside the Homestead where perhaps he lay beside her in her upstairs bedroom as she worked late nights on her poetry, culminating in the prolific 1861–1865 period.

Dickinson wrote a letter to Thomas Wentworth Higginson in January 1866, notifying him quite simply that her dog had died and asking Higginson if he would instruct her now in Carlo's absence. What the poet believed she learned from Carlo is anyone's guess, but perhaps some clues may be found in the fact that the lack of his companionship coincides exactly with a remarkable drop in the poet's productivity (given the extant papers available for study). The poet's growing reluctance to leave the Homestead is probably a natural outcome of the loss of what her father saw as her protector. That Carlo died so soon after she rejoined him at the Homestead after her second long bout of eye treatments in Cambridge must have been especially difficult for her. While certainly there were other good reasons for the shift in the poet's life and work beginning in 1866, the death of her beloved pet ranks with Dickinson scholars as a considerable loss.

MARGARET MAHER

Certainly another factor in the poet's marked decline in productivity in the late 1860s was the loss of the family's Irish domestic employee, Margaret O'Bryan, who married on October 18, 1865. Margaret O'Bryan had begun working for the Dickinsons in the mid-1850s, so she had worked for the family for about eight years by that time. The poet had benefited from her presence in the Homestead as she wrote the bulk of her poems during the Civil War years. With O'Bryan's departure, this free time was not available to the poet until the next maid-of-all-work would be hired a few years later. Like her sister Vinnie, Emily would have been expected to pitch in with her share of the household duties in the absence of hired help. As in the period when they first moved into the Homestead and Mrs. Dickinson had immediately fallen ill, this was another time in the poet's life when she had to bear more of the burden of helping run a household that held such a prominent place in the community.

Having no maid in a house the size of the Homestead was not a small loss. In her article, "Miss Margaret's Emily Dickinson," Aife Murray[1] describes the typical physical labor of running a household the size of the Homestead in the late 1860s. Aside from the arduous tasks of laundering, ironing, and sewing, which may have been hired out, the Dickinson daughters and their mother (or a single maid in their employ) had to maintain heat, light, and clean-water needs for the family, which are taken for granted today. Each room in the Homestead was heated by a Franklin stove. During the day, stoves in each room had to be maintained. This meant adjusting the level of heat, hauling out ashes, and bringing in and stacking new fuel in the form of wood or coal. The cooking stove in the kitchen had to be continually monitored for effects of wind on the fire, which could blow it out at any moment. One of Edward's innovations that he had installed in the Homestead before the 1855 move was the addition of an indoor water pump (to replace the previous need to fetch water from an outside well) and a hearth on which to warm it. Chamber pots or commode chairs had to be emptied each morning and water pitchers refilled in each bedroom.

Light was provided by whale-oil lamps and tallow candles; these also required constant vigilance and maintenance. Lamps had to be cleaned and refilled daily, and the soot they caused all over the house had to be cleaned on a continual basis. The Homestead had many fine furnishings such as marble-top tables and mantles, and white or cream-colored wallpaper in the double parlor. These white surfaces would have collected and shown soot very quickly and would have required constant cleaning. The size of the Homestead would have made just cleaning the soot off all the surfaces a very time-consuming task.

In addition to the daily tasks involving heat, water, light, cooking three square meals a day from scratch, baking, cleaning, and sewing, the changing seasons or other conditions brought about additional duties. These included canning and preparing jams and jellies from harvested fruits (the poet was known for her currant jam), making soap and candles, and planning, preparing for, and cooking holiday meals. Thanksgiving at the Homestead was a feast the poet often commented on as one that the family especially enjoyed. Edward's annual social obligation related to his role as Amherst College treasurer was the commencement tea. The family hosted visiting dignitaries, particularly politicians, on a fairly regular basis as well. In addition to harvesting and social occasions, the women of the nineteenth-century household were also expected to nurse anyone who was ill in the family and do the family mending. There were not a lot of hours left in a day.

One of the roles Dickinson provided throughout her life, whether the Dickinsons hired help or not, was as cook and baker. Edward preferred his eldest daughter's bread to anyone else's, so that meant that she did the daily baking while Vinnie assumed more of the cleaning chores. When they did not have a maid between 1865 and 1869, the poet probably spent more time cleaning than she had for several years previously in addition to her daily baking. This exertion on top of the mental exhaustion and stress she may have experienced from several years of intense, daily writing of her poetic jewels, and long periods of eye strain and treatment in Cambridge, probably explain more than anything else the noticeable decline in writing of this period.

In 1869, the family hired Margaret Maher to work for them as maid-of-all-work. Maher had immigrated from County Tipperary in Ireland during the Great Hunger (famine) of the 1850s. She had worked for the Boltwood family for several years and was about to move to California to live near her brother, when she was hired by Edward Dickinson after her brother urged her to stay in Amherst awhile longer before moving. Although she took the job expecting to stay only a few weeks, Maher ended up staying with the Dickinson family 30 years and outliving not only both of the poet's parents, but also the poet herself, her brother, and her sister.

Maher's contribution to the family over so many years evolved into more than the normally expected physical labor and domestic service. She was a skilled nurse, and both houses counted on her to aid them with the illnesses that befell them. She also grew into an authoritarian figure in the household, at least in the mind of the poet, when it came to running its affairs. As this author has observed from the only known existing correspondence written between the poet and Maher, when Maher was ill at Kelley Square in Amherst, the maid wrote to ask about Mrs. Dickinson's cold when she herself was suffering from the far more serious illness of typhoid fever.[2] The poet wrote about the lack of work getting done by the mischievous ones "Maggie" had left behind, meaning that the poet was probably doing more writing than housework in Maher's absence. Her playfulness and punning in the letter is designed to free her from Maher's disapproval. Margaret Maher and her brother-in-law, Thomas Kelley, who was also a long-term worker for the family, along with several Irish workers employed on the Homestead property, would play crucial roles in the poet's last days and legacy.

HIGGINSON'S VISITS

Although they had corresponded for over eight years, the poet and one of her most important writing mentors, Thomas Wentworth Higginson, finally met face to face in the Homestead on Tuesday, August 16, 1870. When he arrived in town, Higginson sent a note telling Emily he had arrived and wanted to see her. The poet sent a note back saying that through some mix-up she had expected him the day before, but that she would be home that day and would be glad to see him.

Later that evening, around 10 o'clock, Higginson sat down to write his wife about his first face-to-face encounter with his longtime correspondent. The letter is one of the most vivid portrayals of the poet that survive in the written record.[3] Higginson describes the Homestead as a large brick country lawyer's house with a dark parlor. He records that he sent up his card, announcing that he was there, and soon thereafter he heard a pattering step like a child's and then the small woman, at that time not quite 40 years old and about 10 years his junior, glided into the parlor. He described her as a plain woman with no good features, who wore a very clean white dress and a blue shawl. She handed him two day lilies before she

spoke and then said in a breathless voice that the flowers were her introduction. She asked him to forgive her for her fright, that she rarely saw
strangers and was not sure what to say. Higginson goes on to write that she
did not seem to have any trouble talking once she began. She was not
rude; she did stop and ask whether he might have something to add to the
subjects at hand, but then she began talking again quite readily after that.

Her conversation ran over many subjects in his short visit, apparently
filling him in on her own life, which had been of greatest interest to him
for so many years. She told Higginson that she had not learned to tell time
until she was 15 years old, that her father had thought she knew but she
did not. Her father also did not like the family to read anything but the
Bible. She told him that she and Austin and the others had hid books in
the piano and in a bush outside the door so that they might read them.
Her father preferred her bread and she was also pressed upon to make pud-
dings as well. When she was first able to use her eyes again after the long
treatments, she read Shakespeare and marveled at how, if that was the
only book she could read, it would be enough.

She gave Higginson her definition of poetry, which was that when she
reads it, it makes her feel so cold that no fire could warm her. When she
reads it, she told him, she also feels physically like the top of her head has
been taken off. She asked Higginson how so many people in the world got
by each day without having any thoughts, and related to him that, to her,
mere living is joy enough. When he asked her if she wouldn't want to
leave the Homestead grounds and go visiting, she said that she did not desire to leave the Homestead then, nor foresaw any time in the future when
she might possibly wish to do so. To this, she quipped that she feared she
had not expressed her opinion on the issue strongly enough.

Under the pressure of these verbal gymnastics and the mental effort required to keep up with them, Higginson, a veteran colonel of the Civil
War, lasted about an hour. Dickinson gave him a picture of poet Elizabeth
Barrett Browning's tomb that Dr. Holland had given to her. The gesture
was probably quite a sacrificial gift from her to her mentor, considering
how much she admired Browning's poetry. When Higginson was leaving,
the poet expressed her greatest gratitude for his visit, saying that gratitude
was the only secret that could not give itself away. This remark probably
expressed her gratitude to him for all their years of correspondence more
than for his visit. At one time in their letters she had told him that his attention to her writing and faithful correspondence with her about it had
saved her life.

Higginson wrote to his wife that he also saw Edward Dickinson while
he was in town on that trip. He found him to be a stern, nonspeaking gen-

tleman. Higginson wrote that though he thought her father was probably more distant than cruel, he saw what the poet's life had been like in living with him. This impression was perhaps prepared for him by Dickinson's comments about her father the day before. Years later, however, he reflected that he thought the poet's life had been abnormal. That night, Higginson concluded his observation of the encounter in his letter to his wife by confessing that he was glad he did not live closer to the poet; she had drained too much energy out of him. Coming from a man of Higginson's background—editor, essayist, military man, abolitionist—who had connections in several circles in American life and had lived through several tragedies of his own, the comment about Dickinson's ability to drain away energy is noteworthy. Perhaps it is a sign that Dickinson found that she kept friends more easily if she did not expose them to her uncomfortable physical presence too often but instead maintained a cordial written correspondence.

Higginson paid a second and last visit to the poet's home on December 3, 1873, while he was in Amherst to give an invited lecture. Though he does not record the visit in his diary, evidence pieced together from his and the poet's own letters gives the information that is known about the meeting. He reports that her greeting to him was much the same as for his first visit. In a letter, this time to his sisters, Higginson relates that the poet glided into the room, again wearing white and handing him, this time, a *Daphne odora*. A *Daphne odora* is a winter plant that has an exquisite fragrance and is difficult to grow. Under her breath, Higginson relates, the poet asked him how long he was going to stay. From his letter to her following the meeting, readers infer that the poet apparently enjoyed seeing him and never or rarely went out. Higginson indicates that they fell into conversation as old friends. The poet apparently gave him a poem at this meeting—"The Wind begun to rock and Grass," the copy of which was since lost (presumably Higginson misplaced it on, or shortly after, his travels home). Interestingly, in 2003, a rare books and manuscripts dealer put up for sale what he claimed was a missing Dickinson manuscript of this poem for an asking price of $80,000.

Higginson's letter to the poet right after this meeting survives. It is paternal, telling her that he has enjoyed receiving her beautiful thoughts and poems in letters and that he hopes she may always be able to trust him and turn to him for advice. He assures her that he will continue to speak truthfully to her about her poems. Dickinson's letter to him is more cryptic than usual, responding, apparently, to suggestions for reading and other activities in staccato sentences, almost like a list. As a man of letters, Higginson admired and encouraged the poet, but he was also enough of the world to half agree with his wife's comment that the poet was one of the insane who tended to cling to him. He once made the unfortunate comment of calling her a "cracked poetess." Even so, he would continue their steady correspondence for 12 more years. In all, Dickinson would send Higginson 71 letters and 102 poems over 24 years of correspondence.

EDWARD DICKINSON'S DEATH

Six months after Higginson's last visit to see her, Dickinson spent an unusual day with her father. Rather than spend leisure time by herself as she usually did, for some reason, she describes in a letter later, she wanted to be with him, and they spent the afternoon together. Edward, now 71 and an elder statesman, seemed so pleased by their time together that he commented that he wished the afternoon would never end. Nearly embarrassed by this unusual expression of pleasure from him, the poet, herself now 43, suggested when Austin came home, that he and Father go for a walk. The next morning, she woke her father to catch the train to Boston for a meeting of the state legislature. She never saw him again.

Edward felt faint while giving a speech before the General Court in Boston the morning of June 16, 1874. It was a hot day, and the faintness was so strong he had to stop speaking. He retired to his hotel room and called for a doctor. While he had been noticeably tired for some time before this, there had been no indications that he was ill. The doctor gave Edward a dose of morphine, and the poet's father died soon afterward, possibly from the effects of the drug. No family members were present at his death.

The poet describes how she found out about Father's death in a letter to her Norcross cousins. She writes that she and the family were eating dinner when Austin came in holding a message. She could tell by his face that something terrible had happened, but she did not know what. He informed them that Father was very ill, and he and Vinnie had to leave for Boston at once. The train had already left, so the horses were being prepared for the carriage. While this was being done, they all got the news that their father had died.

The day of the funeral, the church was decorated with laurel and other kinds of white flowers. All businesses and shops in Amherst closed in mourning and respect. Mother, Austin and Sue, and Vinnie all attended the funeral, but Emily did not. Her absence at church would not have surprised her father and was not an indication of disrespect or lack of grief. The poet was devastated. Her father's death was the first she endured in her immediate family and the first of the "mighty" deaths she would say later rocked her existence to the core in the 1870s and 1880s. The poet wrote to her cousins that her mind would not come "home" for many days afterward. She wrote to Higginson, telling him that her father's heart was "pure and terrible"[4] and claimed that none other like it ever existed.

While she obviously admired her father greatly during his lifetime and bowed to his wishes in many ways, she had often joked about his rigidity with Austin. For example, after she attended a Jenny Lind concert with her parents and Vinnie, the poet wrote to Austin that Father had sat looking angry and silly the entire time. Apparently, the popular Swedish soprano who sang Taubert's "Bird Song," the "Echo Song," and "Comin' thro' the Rye" among other selections did little to impress Father, or the rest of the family for that matter, in her Northampton concert of July 3, 1851. Dickinson reported that the family seemed more taken with the soprano herself than with her signing. Even as she held him in her highest esteem while he lived, saying that all to him was "real life" and that her views and his of real life often differed, in death, it seems, her father transformed into a more loving and human figure in the poet's imagination.

News of Edward's death appeared in several newspapers across the state. Obituaries and elegies, such as one by Samuel Bowles in the *Springfield Republican*, focused on the steadfastness of his convictions as an old-fashioned Puritan but also on the lack of understanding those he knew always felt toward him and that he appeared to lack about himself. Edward was a paradox; he was the man who sat looking angry all through the Jenny Lind concert but who, in that same year, ran outside to ring the church bells one night when the aurora borealis appeared over Amherst. He didn't want the townspeople to miss seeing it. After working so hard to reestablish the family's good name and to keep a secure and protected household, Edward's standards for himself and others perhaps remained so high that neither he nor anyone else could quite reach them. Despite all of his accomplishments, including fathering a genius American poet and doing so much for the town of Amherst and the state of Massachusetts, the fact that he allowed his search for perfection to separate his humanity from others on a personal level could be regarded as his greatest flaw.

EMILY NORCROSS DICKINSON'S DEATH

The poet lost her mother on November 14, 1882; Emily Norcross Dickinson outlived her husband by eight years. Around the first anniversary of Edward's death seven years earlier, she had suffered a debilitating stroke. Again, what is known about another of the "mighty" deaths the poet would grieve for is known principally through her correspondence, this time in a letter to Elizabeth Holland. She describes her mother as having had a bad cold recently, as had they all, though her mother's weakened constitution took longer to shake it off. The daughters, still caring for their 78-year-old mother after many years of various illnesses, trusted that the doctor would cure her of this common ailment soon enough. They had no cause for alarm. Once her cough went away, she suffered from what the poet described as neuralgia. On the day before her passing, the poet said she seemed much better, eating food, such as custard, ravenously and drinking lemonade and beef tea. The daughters were delighted that her appetite had returned. After a restless night, however, Mrs. Dickinson complained of weariness and was lifted from her bed to her chair earlier than usual. Dickinson describes that her mother took a few short breaths, suddenly asked Vinnie not to leave her, and then passed from this life as though drifting away like a leaf in the wind. The poet made the comment that their mother, who previously could not walk, had flown.

Long-term care of a disabled loved one often results in relief on the part of the caregivers when the loved one passes. The poet, however, who was almost 52 years old when her mother died, grieved her loss deeply. She grew to understand more what her mother had meant to her after her death. As perhaps an unseen foundation that holds up a house is taken for granted, until it crumbles, Mrs. Dickinson's death left an absence in the Homestead that made all three siblings feel orphaned and rudderless to some degree, even though they were all now in middle age. Surprisingly, not much has been written about the matriarch's funeral, but this serves as testament to so many nineteenth-century mothers—and mothers of any period—who nurtured their young quietly and with courage, self-sacrifice, love, and imagination in the deep recesses of the private sphere. The poet does tell in a letter that she and Vinnie had grown perhaps less resistant to their mother's perfectionism in cooking, housekeeping, and other household matters and more affectionate toward her in her later years. Vinnie speaks fondly of their mother's love of bird songs and flowers, which Emily obviously inherited from her. The poet relates that Mrs. Dickinson carried violets to the grave, and her letters of grief show a woman who honored her mother and felt her loss deeply.

JUDGE OTIS PHILLIPS LORD

It is perhaps ironic that readers and scholars spend so much time focusing on the various identities of possible romantic interests in Dickinson's earlier life, when documentation exists that points more definitively to a love affair in her later years. The gentleman was Judge Otis P. Lord, who had been a close friend of her father's for many years. Lord had often visited the Homestead, and perhaps the poet, who had so idolized her father, saw common traits between him and Lord that drew her to find the Judge's character appealing. Added to that, traits, which Edward found attractive in a friend and which offset his own stern personality, may have also appealed to his daughter who was perhaps more like Edward in ways than are generally admitted.

Lord graduated from Amherst College in 1832 when the poet was not yet two years old. While there, he aided in founding the college's first literary society. Earning a law degree at Harvard, Lord practiced law and was elected as a Massachusetts state representative where he served several terms. His friendship with Edward Dickinson began in 1859 when Lord was appointed to the Superior Court. When he visited the Homestead, from his home in Salem, Massachusetts, Lord's wife, Elizabeth Farley, often accompanied him. The couple had no children.

There are theories that Lord and the poet may have fallen in love much before Dickinson's letter expressing these emotions was first addressed to him in the late 1870s. Some argue that Lord is "Master," and that many of the flood period poems of the 1860s are about him as a married man, unreachable to her. There is even some suggestion that Lord visited her secretly when she stayed in Cambridge and was undergoing eye treatments, though documentary evidence about this is scarce and inconclusive. What is clear in the record is that only months after Lord's wife died on December 10, 1877 (ironically, the poet's 47th birthday), Dickinson letters exist that declare the poet's love for Lord. Judge Lord also made frequent visits to the Homestead after this time, as recorded in Austin's diary. He often brought along his niece, Abby Farley. Abby did not approve of her uncle's relationship with the poet, since she feared a late marriage would cost her the large inheritance she expected to receive from her aging, childless uncle. In light of Dickinson's public persona as a recluse—always dressed in virginal white—reading Abby Farley's description of the poet as a loose woman strikes most readers as either shocking or amusing.

Marriage was apparently flirted with as an option, though an unlikely one for these two older adults expressing romantic interest for perhaps the last time in their lives. The year Lord visited Amherst several times he gave the poet the *Complete Concordance to Shakespeare* for Christmas. He was 68, and she was 50.

Perhaps one of the strongest indications that the poet was always more in love with the idea of love that could be expressed in poetry, than she was with the actual complications and changes in one's life that love affairs could bring, is evidenced in her letters following Lord's sudden death in 1884. Perhaps numb from so many severe losses by this time, or perhaps as an indication that she had been playing more than feeling, she seems to accept Lord's death as yet one more added loss and does not appear to grieve for it quite as strongly, or at least as visibly in the record, as for others in her life. She does record, however, that the blows of death were coming one right after the other to her by this time, and she was suffering greatly under the drowning power of them all.

DICKINSON AND CHILDREN

Emily Dickinson's relationship with children was one of the continuous joys of her life. Her appeal for them has not waned from the young people she knew in her lifetime to those of today who like to read her poems at a very young age.[5] The popular stories about her stealing cookies from under Margaret Maher's nose to give to them in secret or lowering gingerbread in a basket down from her window on a rope to them during their play appear to be true. Once, she allowed a neighbor boy, MacGregor Jenkins, into her conservatory to observe a moth. Another time she returned her nephew Ned's boots to The Evergreens on a silver tray with a bouquet of flowers fitted inside each one. She sent a dead bumblebee in a letter with a poem to school with little Gilbert for his teacher, and she remarked about a photograph of Mattie, Austin and Susan's only daughter, that Mattie looked like the girl she had always wanted to be, but wasn't. Children make up a good share of the personae in her poems as well, and she often spoke in letters with nostalgia about the times, oddly, when she was a "boy." Although the poet appears to have had good relationships with all of Austin and Susan's children next door, she had a particular fondness for their youngest son, Gilbert or "Gib," Thomas Gilbert Dickinson. What happened to Gib and its particular importance on her own life in her later years makes his story particularly noteworthy.

EDWARD (NED) DICKINSON

With Ned born in 1861 and Mattie born in 1866, Austin and Susan's first- and second-child's births interestingly bookmark the poet's most productive writing years.

Named after Edward, Ned was the baby the poet was afraid of "joggling," in the letter-poem she sent to Sue. He was first cared for by a succession of nurses as the new parents attempted to adjust to life with an infant crying day and night, possibly from colic or some other problem. These nurses included the aging former slave Louisa Greene Shaw (known as Aunt Abbe, Abba, Aboo, and other names), whom Susan relieved after catching her asleep while holding the baby; Yankee Cerinthia Inghram who left of her own accord claiming that Ned's constant crying was unusual and that there was something wrong with him; and Maggie Conroy of Hartford, who finally seemed to ease Ned's troubles and was a calming, if short-lived influence on the whole family. Ned did suffer from health problems. He was epileptic and did not graduate from Amherst College due to absences because of illness. He got a job as a librarian on campus and was engaged to marry Alice (Alix) Hill when he died in his thirties from angina.

When he was a boy, the poet called herself Uncle Emily in writing to him, and Ned grew to be a witty gentleman much like his grandfather Dickinson and his "uncle." Like his father, he and his aunt shared private jokes. Several books by Charles Dickens bear Ned's name in the Dickinson family library. Ned's notebooks and letters show demonstrable writing skill and careful thought. He outlived his famous aunt by several years and came to see her poetry published in books, and he outlived his father as well, but his mother would have to bury him in 1898, with only one child of her three remaining.

MARTHA (MATTIE) GILBERT DICKINSON BIANCHI

The poet's only niece, Martha (Mattie) Gilbert Dickinson Bianchi, brought pleasure to both households. It was Mattie and her friends who stood under the poet's window and begged for gingerbread, knowing they would soon see the basket lowered in their direction with the tasty treat inside. Bright and articulate, Martha recalled later being allowed into the poet's room on Sundays while both families went off to church. She recalled her aunt's explanation of the solitude she so enjoyed. Turning an invisible key above Martha's head that would lock her door from the inside, the poet told her in a conspiring voice that locking oneself in one's room meant "freedom" from the outside world. Though she studied music at Smith College, Martha grew up to be an accomplished writer and poet herself. In the early twenty-first century, her work on her memoirs of her aunt, her aunt's biography, poems, and letters, however, were remembered longer than any of her own writings. She traveled widely in Europe and elsewhere and married "Count" Alexander Bianchi in 1902. However, she divorced him in 1920 after he was convicted of financial fraud charges (he was not really a member of the Russian royalty as he'd claimed either), and he had abandoned the marriage.

Having no children, Martha took her role as the last member of the Dickinson family line seriously and conscientiously, preserving many of her aunt's and her family's papers and artifacts in The Evergreens after selling the Homestead to ease the financial strain of maintaining both houses. Bianchi died in 1943; interestingly, she was born just after the Civil War and died during World War II. Her contributions to the Dickinson legacy and her own writing and charity work establish Martha as another Dickinson who deserves more study.

THOMAS GILBERT (GIB) DICKINSON

Gilbert was born August 1, 1875, a year after the poet's father died, and as she was trying to recover from the first crucial blow to the immediate family. Perhaps it was the timing of his birth, a joyful moment in the midst of such grief, or the fact that the poet herself, like Susan, would be 45 years old the year the boy was born and could perhaps enjoy him with the pleasure of middle-age maturity; or perhaps it was the boy's own charming personality that would soon become evident, or some combination of these factors. In any case, of all those she had known in the family and in the neighborhood in the years before, Gilbert Dickinson arguably became the most important child in the poet's life.

In a handwritten mother's journal yet unpublished,[6] Susan Dickinson describes the day of Gib's birth as a pleasant Sunday morning. Through the open windows and doors, she could hear music from the Congregational Church, which Austin had helped see built, almost directly across Main Street. She heard their neighbors, the Sweetsers, walking home from services on the shortcut between the Dickinson houses approved for them by the families. Gib was born around noon. He was a sizeable baby and was taken care of soon after his birth by the family nurse.

Susan explains that Gib was named Thomas Gilbert Dickinson in honor of her father and brother, but soon the name Thomas was dropped in family use in favor of Gilbert; often this name was shortened to Gib. Among the boy's belongings still housed at The Evergreens is a note he signed "Gilly." In her journal, Susan records the first of several expressions the boy would make that would charm her and her sister-in-law next door. Showing what she called early signs of the "Dickinson will," Gib went toddling through the grass one day. When his mother suggested that he do something, he shrugged his shoulders and trotted off, answering, "No. no. do. mind. to."[7] Clearly charmed by his use of words, Aunt Emily later recorded other things he said in her letters.

There are accounts of the poet watching little Gilbert play in a wash-tub in The Evergreens driveway and others of her delight in his particular manner of speaking. Gilbert's charm was unique in a child so young. As he grew older, he rode his velocipede up and down Main Street, and even the townspeople were quite taken with his interest in them and the world around him. With the next oldest sibling, Mattie, eight years his senior, Gilbert was growing up in a household of older people who no doubt in-dulged him, partly out of their sense of loss for his grandfather. However, Gilbert apparently showed more of the positive than the negative signs of this indulgence.

One of the effects of Austin's long-term interest in landscaping was his influence in the establishment of the Amherst Common. This was a grassy area in the center of town that people could use as a park. Despite several efforts to fill it in, the common was marred by the continual sink-ing of a central portion that had once been a frog pond. This hollow spot continually filled with water, leaving more mud than grass.

In October of 1883, Gilbert and his friends were playing in the mud at Amherst Common, when Gib felt ill and feverish. Back home at The Ever-greens, the doctor diagnosed Gib as having a sudden virulent attack of ty-phoid fever caught from playing in the mud. A few days later, at only eight years old, the boy lay dying. Aunt Emily came over from the Homestead to stay with him, and a bedside vigil began. During the night, Gilbert's face suddenly brightened, and he appeared to be seeing a vision of a door opening and someone there waiting for him. Then he died.

The poet was so stricken by the scene, perhaps bringing back memories from Sophia Holland's deathbed years ago when she was a girl, that she immediately fell ill herself and had to be walked home to the Homestead in the middle of the night. Gilbert's tragic, untimely death was a blow from which the entire family would never fully recover. Austin and Emily, in particular, would respond to it in ways that changed the Dickinson legacy forever.

MABEL LOOMIS TODD

In 1881, two years before Gilbert's tragic death, a woman in her mid-twenties moved to Amherst. Her husband was Professor David Peck Todd, who was to teach astronomy at Amherst College, and the woman was Mabel Loomis Todd; they had married five years before. They brought with them their new baby daughter, Millicent, who was the only child the couple would ever have.

Mrs. Todd was young, vivacious, and full of curiosity, talent, and ambition. She had the ability to make herself the center of attention wherever she went. As a new faculty wife, she soon made the rounds of Amherst society, and commented about the mythic poet whom she heard lived at the brick Homestead on Main Street. It wasn't long before her energy, talent, and new connections resulted in her being invited there to play the piano and sing for the unseen poet upstairs. By 1882, she had managed to infatuate 53-year-old Austin Dickinson, who was apparently ripe for a midlife affair. With the death of his father a few years earlier and the increased responsibility of a new, third child, all of the Dickinson heritage now rested heavily upon his shoulders—and Austin had never been quite the man of conviction that his father was. Not having to struggle in the same way that his father had when he was younger, Austin had never had this level of responsibility and burden of duties before.

Despite the new baby, strains in Susan and Austin's marriage were beginning to become more serious. Austin was growing tired of Susan's efforts at maintaining the family's public persona, finding the extravagance of some of her projects increasingly hollow and the expense unnecessary. The social scene she had worked so diligently to cultivate was beginning to pale in Austin's growing preference for quieter moments and time for reflection, more like those his sister enjoyed. Sue probably sensed Austin's emotional withdrawal, but was perhaps hurt by his growing lack of interest and involvement (perhaps echoing his mother's reserve) and was also immersed in her three children, house, writing, and entertaining. During disagreements, it appears that Sue's natural temper flared, and Austin retreated across the lawn to the quiet of the Homestead. Problems got increasingly buried beneath layers of resentment and lack of communication rather than being aired out and resolved.

By contrast, vivacious Mabel Todd, only 26 and growing more infatuated with the country lawyer, became more sympathetic to his frustrations by the day and was a welcome refuge to Austin, who enjoyed her attention. The scenario is an old one. He and Mabel admitted their attraction for one another on a walk on September 11, 1882, a day mysteriously noted as "Rubicon" in Austin's diary. They began to exchange a series of passionate love letters.

Gilbert's death in October 1883 was a crushing blow to Susan, Austin, and Emily as well as to the entire family. As sometimes happens, a tragedy can break an already strained relationship, and this is what happened when Austin left Susan in the midst of her grief and sought comfort with Mabel in the form of a clandestine rendezvous at the Homestead in December 1883. After that, Austin's old romanticism rekindled much as it was when he and Susan each ate a chestnut at vespers in the evening in remembrance of one another during their courting days. He wrote his and Mabel's names commingled on two pieces of paper, "amuasbteiln." He kept one copy in his wallet, and she kept the other in her diary.

Their relationship became a long-term affair that settled into such a comfortable routine that eventually both Susan Dickinson and David Todd were aware of it. Although Susan, for her part, is on record as confronting Austin for his betrayal, neither Susan nor David left their cheating spouses, choosing instead to bear the pain of the affair rather than disrupt their families. Apparently, the privacy of the Homestead and the Todd home, the Dell, offered the two the discretion they needed to keep proof of the affair off-limits to Amherst society. David Todd became not only tolerant but complicit with the affair over time. His daughter, Millicent Todd Bingham, later recalled his whistling a tune from *Martha* when he would return late at night from the observatory as a cue to the lovers that he was approaching. Years later, David suffered a mental breakdown and had to be institutionalized.

A draft letter exists that Austin once considered leaving Amherst for Omaha, presumably to start a new life with Mabel, but the letter was apparently never mailed. While there was undoubtedly gossip that Austin and Susan's marriage was under strain and that Austin was drawn to Mabel's company, there seems to be little suggestion that the Dickinson's carefully guarded integrity was questioned openly in the community.

While the poet never met her, Todd was at the Homestead quite frequently to be with Austin, play the piano, and sing. It is not known what the poet thought of her or of her brother's relationship with a mistress, but hints in documents suggest that she either disapproved but did not confront Austin or that she abstained from having a view altogether, preferring to let matters of the heart be private to the people concerned.

For her part, Todd seemed boundless in creative energy. She liked to paint, and she frequently painted flowers and designs as accents on collars and cuffs and other parts of her dresses as well as on the walls of the Dell. She presented little framed pieces to people as gifts. She painted one such piece for the poet, a set of Indian pipes, a fungus like plant that the poet had expressed an interest in because of its rarity and ghostly, translucent white color. Because the poet reportedly liked it, the painting later became the cover of the first three volumes of Dickinson's poetry ever published.

That Mabel Todd came into the Dickinsons' lives so late and caused such a disruption, when she was young, and they were all middle aged, would be sad for the families but perhaps less important to scholars had she not played the role she did in the publication of the poems after the poet's death. In a move that must have torn apart Susan Dickinson, who had loved the poet as a dear friend, sister, and possibly more for so many decades, Lavinia took away the manuscripts she had entrusted to her care for publication and gave a portion of them to Todd. Believing she had both the poet's siblings on her side, Todd set about preparing the manuscripts with a sense of free rein.

Mabel and Austin remained completely devoted to one another until Austin's death in 1895, well after the first two books of his sister's poems had appeared in print. Some scholars believe Mabel was Austin's true love and sustained the poet's two siblings through the trials of their later years and that she did a service to the world by working with the poet's manuscripts as well as promoting them as diligently as she did. Other scholars point to the silenced voice of the wronged woman, Susan Dickinson, as well as the soured relationship between Mabel and Vinnie over a piece of land after Austin's death. Opponents to Mabel's entering the scene see her as a home-wrecking other woman who was out for her own fame and notoriety, both by seducing Austin Dickinson away from his wife and family and by getting involved in his sister's poetic legacy. What is true about both of these views of this multitalented late-nineteenth-century woman is that Mabel Loomis Todd, whether from love or from self-interest or both, became an important part of the poet's story.

LAST DAYS

Dickinson never fully recovered from the "nervous prostration" she was diagnosed with after Gilbert's death in the fall of 1883. On June 14, she collapsed while baking a cake with Margaret Maher in the Homestead kitchen. The fainting episodes increased, giving her family much concern. By the fall of 1885, the recurring episodes and the frailty of her health in between them made Vinnie barely allow herself out of Emily's sight. She took up a bedside vigil following each fainting episode, worrying that the worst may happen at any moment. In November, Austin cancelled a trip to Boston and relieved Vinnie at Emily's bedside from time to time during the spells. Neighbors indicated that were it not for Vinnie's careful vigilance after each episode, Emily may have died as much as a year earlier than she did.

Sometime in May 1886, Dickinson wrote her last letter that survives. She wrote to her Norcross cousins, then approximately 44 and 39 years old. Even in their middle age, Emily still thought of them as the girls she knew during family visits and as the young women she stayed with during her eye treatments in Cambridge. About a year before she wrote this last letter she had read a popular novel titled *Called Back* by Hugh Conway. Dickinson had thought the novel "impressive" and the story "haunting." In the story, the blind narrator overhears a murder. He recovers his sight later on and marries a beautiful but detached woman who has many mysteries in her past. When they return to the scene of the murder in the chapter "Called Back," suddenly the woman connects with her husband by remembering her brother's murder on that spot, and the narrator sees flashes of the scene that he overheard years earlier rise up from his wife's repressed memories each time she takes his hand. As a result, her psychological healing can begin and the mystery for the husband is solved when he locates the killer in a Siberian prison. In her last letter, Dickinson wrote, "Little Cousins, Called back. Emily."[8] Whether the phrase referred to her knowledge of how serious her failing health was becoming or not, readers have almost always read the letter, the last one she ever wrote, as a premonition.

Austin records in his diary for May 13, 1886, that he had just finished watching over the planting of azaleas and rhododendrons on the grounds and was about to head off to his law office in town when Vinnie came to tell him that Emily was not feeling well. He decided to stay home within easy reach. Sometime around 10 o'clock that morning, Emily slipped into unconsciousness. The doctor was called and stayed with her most of the afternoon, but as of six o'clock that evening when Austin was writing his diary entry, she had not yet awakened. She remained unconscious all that night and all the next day. Austin described her last moments in his diary. He relates that the family determined during the night of May 14 that Emily would not likely survive the following day, or as he put it, that "Emily would not wake again this side."[9] Austin records May 15 as a terrible day of many hours listening to his sister's labored breathing. Finally, just before the whistles sounded for six o'clock in the evening of May 15, she stopped breathing altogether. Austin records that when it happened Vinnie was sitting with Mrs. Montague and Mrs. Jameson, and that he was close by.

Dr. Orvis F. Bigelow wrote "Bright's disease" as the cause of death and indicated that the poet had suffered from the kidney ailment for two-and-a-half years, or from the time of Gilbert's death. Today, analyzing evidence in letters and other documents that describe the poet's symptoms, Dr. Norbert Hirschhorn and scholar Polly Longsworth have concluded that Dr. Bigelow may have written down Bright's disease because he really was not quite sure of the cause. The medical knowledge of the time most likely could not explain what was wrong with her. Today, Dickinson's symptoms suggest that the poet may have been suffering from severe primary hypertension. The months of fainting episodes and the brief coma from which she never awoke, together with her high-strung emotional makeup and the stress she lived under from grieving the loss of at least 31 friends and relatives who died in her lifetime just from tuberculosis,[10] not to mention deaths, like Gib's, from other causes. All this combined make it appear that Dickinson died from untreated high blood pressure leading to a fatal stroke. It is difficult to imagine what poetry may have yet been produced by her genius had she lived in a time when she could have had her symptoms regulated, as is possible today, through regular checkups, monitoring, and modern-day prescriptions.

It was Susan who made the arrangements to prepare the body for burial. The body was embalmed by Ellery Strickland, an Amherst mortician, then wrapped in a white flannel robe reportedly made by Eunice R. Powell. Violets and cypripedium were placed at her throat and two heliotropes put in her hand. She was laid in a white casket in the hallway of the beloved Homestead. Strickland said she looked younger than her 55 years, with her abundant auburn hair showing no gray whatsoever. Thomas Wentworth Higginson also viewed the body and commented on its youthfulness, the lack of gray hair and no wrinkles on the face. Higginson said the poet looked 30 years old, which is not far from the age she was when she sent him the first four poems for his consideration in 1862. It is almost as though her poetry kept her young.

The funeral, held on May 19 in the Homestead library, was brief. Reverend George S. Dickerman, the new minister at the Congregational Church, read from I Corinthians 15. Following a prayer, Thomas W. Higginson read Emily Brontë's last poem, one that Emily Dickinson loved, "No Coward Soul Is Mine." After this short ceremony, four honorary pallbearers, including Doc Hitchcock, the president of Amherst College, John Jameson, and Dwight Hills, carried her coffin on a special brier made for this purpose out of the library, down the hall, and to the back door of the Homestead.

The poet had left specific instructions for her funeral procession, which Austin made sure were followed. Her chosen six pallbearers were all Irish workers from the Homestead whom she had seen regularly and had come to know in and around the grounds for many years. They were Thomas Kelley, Dennis Scannell, Dennis Cashman, Daniel Moynihan, Patrick Ward, and Stephen Sullivan. Townspeople who found out about it later thought the request unusual, and perhaps the workers' help was solicited based on the uncommon procession that was to follow instead of the usual carriage. Since then, however, the poet's choice of these pallbearers has been interpreted as a tribute to the Irish people who worked faithfully and well for her family for so many years. Her instructions directed that the six men carry her, not out the front door and down the street to a carriage and a public funeral procession down Main Street, but instead out the back door of the Homestead, through the garden, straight through the barn with its doors wide open in front and back, and across three meadows whose fences had been lowered in the areas needed for her to cross, on to the family burial plot in West Cemetery. The procession went this way not only to maintain her privacy, but also to keep her always within view of the house.

Dickinson remains resting now in the family plot surrounded by a wrought-iron fence in Amherst's West Cemetery between her sister Lavinia (who died in 1899) on her right, and her parents on the left. Her paternal grandparents are buried to the left of her parents. The poet is buried in the same cemetery she watched funeral processions go into as a young girl from her window at the West Street house. While a plain, brick-type marker of the period bearing only her initials, "E.E.D." signified the grave for many years, the poet's niece, Martha Dickinson Bianchi, placed tall gravestones for all of the family in the plot in the twentieth century. Emily's now reads: "Emily Dickinson Born Dec. 10, 1830 Called Back May 15, 1886."

Devotion to the poet's burial place is strong even in the twenty-first century. Each year on or around May 15, there is a poetry walk from the Homestead to the gravesite where participants gather in tribute and read favorite poems. One frequent visitor reports seeing at least one simple bouquet or single blossom on her grave every day she has visited, in all seasons of the year. A friend of twentieth-century poet Robert Francis, who says the poet loved Dickinson dearly, went so far as to sprinkle some of his ashes on her grave in a private ritual, bringing the two Amherst poets together in "adjoining rooms."[11] Even a graveyard Web site, which shows photographs of gravestones of prominent people and hosts personal messages to them from online visitors, contained nearly 100 heartfelt, personal messages to the poet beneath the image of her grave in spring 2003. The poet who wrote so much about the death she witnessed all around her in nineteenth-century New England and who imagined in her lifetime as much as anyone before or since what it might be like to be dead, bears the remembrance in that state of a devoted following.

NOTES

1. Murray, "Miss Margaret," pp. 715–720.
2. See Connie Ann Kirk, " 'I will sone be home': Margaret Maher, Emily Dickinson, and an Irish Trunk Full of Poems," in *Ireland's Great Hunger: Silence,*

Memory, and Commemoration, ed. David Valone and Christine Kinealy (Lanham, MD: University Press of America, 2002).

3. Thomas Wentworth Higginson letter to Mary Higginson, qtd. in Dickinson, *Letters,* Johnson, ed., 3 vols., # 342a.

4. Dickinson letter to Thomas Wentworth Higginson, July, 1874 (Dickinson, *Letters,* Johnson, ed., 3 vols.).

5. See Connie Ann Kirk, "Why Do Children Like Emily Dickinson?" *Emily Dickinson International Society Bulletin* 12, no. 1 (May/June 2000).

6. Susan Gilbert Dickinson, Unpublished journal, The Evergreens. Courtesy of the Martha Dickinson Bianchi Trust.

7. Susan Gilbert Dickinson, Unpublished journal, The Evergreens. Courtesy of the Martha Dickinson Bianchi Trust.

8. Dickinson letter to Louise and Frances Norcross, May, 1886 (Dickinson, *Letters,* Johnson, ed., 3 vols.).

9. Qtd. in Sewall, *Life,* p. 125.

10. Habegger, *"Wars,"* pp. 640–41.

11. Lecture, "Emily Dickinson: An Appreciation," Jones Library, Amherst, MA, April 24, 2003.

Chapter 10

"FLUID TEXT" AND THE PROBLEM OF EDITING

Vinnie discovered the poems in 1886, in the bottom drawer of Emily's cherry bureau, following her sister's death. There may have been more poems in Margaret Maher's trunk, as the maid claimed later. Since that day, the problem of what to do with the poems hasn't been so much whether or not to publish them (a matter on which all of the major editors over the years have agreed) but how best to present Dickinson's writing in a manner that is meaningful and respectful of the way in which it was left by the poet. Since the poet did not title the poems, date them, gather her portfolios into any particular order that is apparent, or otherwise prepare the poems for publication herself, every editor has found them problematic. In the early years right after her death first editors transcribed them by hand from the original manuscripts. Now editors are digitizing the manuscripts into images that can be put online, studied by anyone with internet access, and even searched by keywords. From the earliest efforts until now, every editor has had to think of issues such as what to include and why, how to arrange what gets included, what to correct or change and why, and many other issues. From the beginning, the editing of Emily Dickinson's poems has not only been difficult but also the source of controversy.

One of the additional problems the poet left behind was that many of the manuscripts are in the form one might call a work in progress. This means that words are crossed out, several word variants are suggested at the bottoms of pages, line breaks are inconsistent from one copy of a poem to another; genres are unclear from letter-poems to poems included in letters, to poems alone, and vice versa. The poet did not make final choices for publication about these matters. The uncertainties of the texts make them difficult to manage, and editors find they must explain their rationale each time a new edition of the poems or letters appears, as well as explain why they believe a major new edition is necessary in the first place. Therefore, the text of most Dickinson poems is not *fixed*. If it were fixed, it would mean that the poet had made her own final choices and prepared final drafts for print. Instead, as a group, the manuscripts are a *fluid text*.

In their inaugural first editions, the series of the first three books with the Indian pipes on the covers, Mabel Loomis Todd and Thomas Wentworth Higginson did not attempt to be chronological but instead grouped the poems into themes such as nature, death, love, immortality, and so forth. The poems were changed heavily in terms of punctuation, capitalization, rhyme, spelling, line and stanza breaks, and other matters. In many ways, the poems in the first three editions are nearly unrecognizable from the original manuscripts. These publications probably mark the extreme in terms of heavy handedness in editing. Millicent Todd Bingham's editions, edited with her mother, followed much the same format or incorporated a numbering system.

Martha Dickinson Bianchi, the poet's niece, and her assistant Alfred Leete Hampson, attempted to provide a bit of biographical context to the letters. Martha prepared a biographical section for the front of her edition. In it she published letters not in the possession of Todd. Also, Martha and Hampson were the first to attempt to publish the complete poems. To this edition were added those poems that Vinnie had not given to Todd, and over which a legal dispute with Todd resulted in neither side having the complete manuscripts with which to work. While Bianchi's editions provided new poems and letters that had not before been seen, there was still no real complete set of the poems and letters available.

In 1955, Thomas H. Johnson had all of the extant papers available to him with which to work. He assembled them in what he determined to be chronological order by carefully studying Dickinson's handwriting and other characteristics of the manuscripts that would help date them, such as matching handwriting and subject matter to letters that were dated. He also went back to the manuscripts and restored many of the line breaks, capitalizations, and perhaps most noteworthy at the time, Dickinson's punctuation—restoring her frequent use of the dash that now so characterizes her poems. He produced the first three-volume variorum edition of the poems and another three-volume edition of the letters. As the first editor to assemble all of the extant Dickinson materials together in a single set of volumes, Johnson's work was a groundbreaking achievement in Dickinson scholarship. His single-volume reading edition, which is still available in hardcover and in paperback, presents a single edited version of each poem that was still in popular use in colleges and universities and by general readers in 2004.

In the 1990s, Ralph W. Franklin observed that Johnson's efforts at putting the poems into chronological order had not taken into account that the poet did not leave them this way. Years ago, presumably Vinnie, Mabel Loomis Todd, and Thomas Wentworth Higginson had separated the poems from the original portfolio packets Dickinson had sewn and laid them out separately in order to arrange them in a new order by theme. Unfortunately, the early editors left no record of what was where before they untied packets and began separating pages. Franklin went back to the original manuscripts and toiled with great effort to reorder them—not chronologically as Johnson had done, nor by theme as Todd and Higginson had done—but by the order in which Dickinson left them in her dresser drawer. Franklin examined features such as handwriting like Johnson had, but he also analyzed elements of the paper such as folds, soiling, matching pinholes, the appearance of handwriting across sheets of paper in conjunction with one another, ink, pen strokes, and other factors. Franklin's resulting two-volume facsimile edition of the manuscripts was another monumental feat in Dickinson scholarship. For the first time, readers could see images of the original manuscripts, examine markings the poet left behind on the pages, pinholes, stationery embossments, doodles, pen strokes, and the like. Seeing the poems this way has promoted the fluid text approach to reading and interpreting the poems by presenting them with their variants intact, something Johnson did not do. Franklin went beyond the facsimile edition as well when he attempted to convert the manuscripts to print with elaborate codes as to how the words appear on the original pages and what variants appear at the bottom and in the margins of sheets. He published a three-volume variorum edition of the manuscripts in print. In addition, he edited a single-volume reader's edition that makes choices among poem variants easier and more enjoyable for general readers because the entries are devoid of their scholarly apparatus. Although the Franklin edition is now considered the standard edition by many scholars, the single-volume reading copy was not yet available in paperback in 2004. A paperback edition is almost a necessity for an edition to be widely accepted in courses for college undergraduates.

Still later, Martha Nell Smith and Ellen Louise Hart edited Emily's letters and letter-poems to Susan Dickinson by honoring as best they could within the confines in print, the line breaks and word variants appearing in the original manuscripts. Smith and the other general editors of the online *Dickinson Electronic Archives*, took Franklin's work one step further.

Working from Susan Dickinson's original dilemma of how to present the poems and letters in a way that frees them from the confines of the printed book entirely, Smith and her colleagues are systematically digitizing the images of original Dickinson poems and letters as well as other papers belonging to the Dickinson family. The result lends more of a portfolio or workshop appearance to the presentation that more closely resembles the way the poet may have sorted through her drawer or trunk in search of poems. For example, letters are searchable by correspondent or by keyword or chronology; the choice is up to the reader. The electronic edition honors the role of the reader as a participant in the reading of the fluid text and thus perhaps best illustrates how Dickinson's manuscripts shall ever remain a work in progress.

NOMENCLATURE FOR THE POEMS AND LETTERS

Since so few of the poems were titled, nomenclature for the poems has also changed with the various editions. Beginning with Johnson, the poems and letters were identified from each other by a numbering system that followed Johnson's established chronology. In this way, a poem in the Johnson edition would be noted by a J number, for example, J 29, and a letter by a similar notation such as L 41. Similarly, a poem from the Franklin print edition would be noted by its Fr number, which usually is a different number for the same poem than the Johnson number. An Fr number would look like Fr 35. The *Fr* was used instead of the *F* alone, because in some cases, *F* came to stand for fascicle number, or the number assigned to the manuscript booklet (meaning the grouping of poems sewn together by Dickinson) based on Franklin's criteria. The letters and letter-poems to Susan Dickinson were collected in *Open Me Carefully*, and these are sometimes referred to with an OMC number, such as OMC 32.

Scholars have typically gone two routes to work toward developing some form of standardization of nomenclature in light of the various editions and the more recent emphasis on the original manuscripts. One is to refer to poems by their storage location in drawers and boxes at various university and public-library holdings. In this nomenclature, something like H 82 would not be unusual to see in parentheses underneath a poem. Probably ahead of this trend is the movement toward using first lines of the poems and letters as they appear in the original manuscripts as titles or as a substitute means of identification.

When referring to Dickinson poems in writing, students and scholars alike must take care to be clear which edition they are using and consider that readers may have to look up poems in their own different editions.

Sometimes, for example, scholars provide both J and Fr numbers (though the actual appearance of the poem on the page may be slightly different between the two). The Franklin editions provide a cross-reference between the Johnson numbers and the Franklin numbers in the appendix, but this intermediate step in finding poems under discussion can be distracting and time-consuming. Providing first lines (so far every edition has an index in the back of these) is probably the safest nomenclature system to use combined with a note somewhere in the text or following the paper or article indicating which edition the author is using in his/her discussion.

Chapter 11

MYTHS, MYSTERIES, AND CONTROVERSIES

The mythmaking about Emily Dickinson probably began even before she had left the Homestead for the last time on the shoulders of her father's Irish workmen. Austin's children were told to protect their aunt from town gossip by never revealing anything about her ways, which the family found acceptable and normal for her but that might be deemed out of the ordinary by townsfolk. What had the townspeople heard that drew their suspicions and wagging tongues? They talked about how reclusive she was, which they knew firsthand from not seeing her around town. Not seeing her in society made the stories grow in proportion and kind. Emily was a mystic, they said; she was depraved and immoral; she was insane; too frail for this world—the stories grew and multiplied, most especially from those who were jealous of the Dickinson family's influence or who despised their power in the community and their apparent arrogance about having that power.

Even in the early twenty-first century, after over a quarter of a century of feminist scholarship has done much to unearth possible explanations for why the poet lived the way she did, mysteries and controversies still abound. These mysteries and controversies include the poet's reclusiveness; the three now-famous letters she wrote to someone she addressed as "Master"; her proclivity for wearing the color white; a series of conflicts called the "war between the houses," which involved entanglements over her manuscripts and legacy; the mutilation and apparent censorship of Emily's papers; and the various photograph and manuscript claims.

THE RECLUSE

The first and foremost mystery most people wonder about remains why Dickinson chose not to leave the Homestead and Evergreens grounds after about 1869 or possibly before. Readers form their visions of the recluse from local town folklore, her own letters, and the letters and other writings of people who knew the poet during her lifetime. In her May 11, 1869, letter to Thomas Wentworth Higginson, for example, Dickinson states that she cannot accept his invitation to visit him in Boston because she does not cross her father's ground "to any house or town." Some have read this statement as a sign of severe agoraphobia, or fear of the marketplace that keeps its sufferers in the house, terrified of going out. That the poet did not see her poems into print and called publication an "auction of the mind" could also point to this fear of the marketplace and the public sphere.

Others see this tendency to stay home as a natural shyness growing more intense over time. When one doesn't have to go out and interact with others, a tendency to avoid people may grow into a habit that is difficult to break. Shyness may develop into anxiety about social contact. When visitors came to the Homestead, the poet did refuse to see some of them out of some degree of shyness. At one point, the family dressmaker had to measure Vinnie for Emily's clothes, and the doctor had to speak to her about her symptoms from another room. She liked to remain upstairs and listen to conversations down below or to the playing of the piano. At times, she sent a flower or a poem or a card down on a tray so that the visitor would not leave feeling offended for not having seen her. Yet, there were many visitors to the Homestead the poet did engage with, so this shyness, or game playing, or perhaps even mythmaking of her own design was not universally employed. The poet selected her own society.

Still others see Dickinson as firmly under the thumb of her overprotective father. It may be difficult to imagine Edward, so devoted to the public sphere and working so hard to make a mark in it for the family, refusing to allow his daughter to venture out at all. There is little evidence of any of the women in his family—particularly the two Emilies—having much of a public presence throughout Amherst. Mrs. Dickinson was likely out more than extant records indicate. However, Edward definitely thought a woman's place was in the home, quite literally. Perhaps it was an intense desire on her part to please her father that kept the poet there.

Another explanation may be that the written record is simply too sketchy to show the times she did go out. There are times when tracings of her appear unexpectedly. For example, in her letter to Margaret Maher, the

Dickinson maid who was away from the Homestead ill at Kelley Square, the poet mentions going out for "black" to the store, perhaps shoe black. This may also have been a joke about wearing mourning clothes during Margaret's absence. Emily's signature turns up on legal documents as a witness for her family's transactions. These may have been signed at the Homestead, but more likely they would have been signed in her father's law office downtown, where presumably all parties to the legal transaction would have been present simultaneously for the signing of the document. Possibly the trouble with shaping a realistic picture of the poet's comings and goings is that she went out infrequently enough to leave few written tracings of her movements, thus developing a justified reputation for staying home. However, perhaps she was not the total recluse who never left the grounds at all, which family members and others who knew her characterized her as being—and that readers have taken so literally.

THE "MASTER" LETTERS

Still another mystery that continues to baffle scholars is the collection of three letters she wrote and probably did not mail that were found among her papers after she died. All three are intimate and puzzling letters, written to an unnamed person or being, whom she addresses only as "Master." The first one is dated by editor Thomas Johnson as spring 1858. In this letter, she seems to be responding to either a letter written to her or to a conversation she had previously with the addressee. She is sad that "Master" is ill, and she is ill as well, but she will keep her hand working to write the letter to reach out to him/her. She writes about the Sabbath and the sea and her flowers and the hills. It is difficult to decipher what the letter may mean because so much of it references a letter or conversation to which present-day readers are not privy.

The second "Master" letter is dated by biographer Richard B. Sewall as January 1861. It is a letter of longing, of wishing she and the addressee could be together. The narrator of the letter calls herself Daisy. Again, the conversation is intimate, full of images that probably only the addressee could follow. Some readers suggest that words in this letter such as "presbyteries" point to Charles Wadsworth as a candidate for "Master." Others look at clues like "beard," which they say suggests the addressee is the effervescent editor of the *Springfield Republican* and friend of her brother's, Samuel Bowles. The last letter is dated by editor Thomas Johnson as early 1862. Again, the narrator calls herself Daisy. She seems to be apologetic for an offense she fears she has caused "Master" and longs for them to be together again.

It is not clear whether fair copies of the letter drafts found after her death were ever actually mailed. It is also not clear that they are really letters and not works of epistolary fiction. Some have argued that they are not technically addressed to any single individual but rather to an imaginary conglomeration of people who occupied this place of admiration and love in her mind. She did call Thomas Wentworth Higginson "Master" in at least one letter that is known, but her first correspondence with him postdates the dating of all three mystery letters. Suggestions in the guessing game have run the gamut from God to her father to Austin to her sister-in-law Sue, to Wadsworth, Bowles, and Judge Otis P. Lord to no one in particular, to someone in her imagination. On and on, the speculation and attempts at proof go. For some more recently in the scholarship, the speculation has become tiresome because of the lack of definitive proof for any one argument and most especially because of the realization that identifying "Master" would probably not give as much insight into the poet and her work as one might hope. The question is older than the Pelham hills in Dickinson scholarship and many scholars now avoid the puzzle of "Master's" identity altogether and move on to what they find to be more interesting mysteries. Still, a scholar or historian who could somehow prove "Master's" true identity would solve one of the greatest mysteries in American literature.

THE WOMAN IN WHITE

Just as Dickinson was said to never go out after a certain period, she is also said to have always worn white from about the same period in the 1860s on, or especially from after her father's death in 1874. These accounts are told by different people who saw her wearing white or who commented on her habit of wearing white. When he visited in the early 1870s, Thomas Wentworth Higginson said the poet was wearing an exquisitely white pique dress with a blue shawl. Mabel Loomis Todd said that Austin told her she wore white after their father died, perhaps as some kind of reverse mourning garb. The only surviving garment of the poet's is an all-white dress that has been recently copied and placed on display in the Homestead at the Emily Dickinson Museum while the original was put away in storage to preserve it. The poet's body was wrapped in a white flannel robe for burial, and observers said her coffin was white. Whiteness appears in the letters and in the poetry, but what Dickinson thought about it in relation to her clothing is difficult to discern and has raised more questions and speculations than answers.

As with the "Master" letters, speculations based on the assumption that the poet only wore white have run a wide range. One idea is that Dickinson saw herself as a nun or priestess wearing a habit to show devotion to her poetry or to a forbidden or failed love affair, or perhaps to symbolize her purity of purpose. More practical ideas suggest that white was easier to wash because there was no fear of colors bleeding, or that she wore white because she was allergic to the dyes in nineteenth-century clothing. Still another idea suggests that "Master," or some other person, liked her appearance when she "came to him in white," so that she wore that color to please that person out of a lifelong devotion, whether or not that person was around to see her wearing white or any other color.

If there was nothing more to it than personal preference, perhaps her habit, if indeed there was one, was simply born of practicality for the lifestyle she chose of working at home. Wearing the same color eliminated one more tedious decision for her every morning and could, perhaps, keep her focused on what she believed were more important choices to make in one's day. Those who wear uniforms to work or school often tell of how much easier and simpler this makes their morning routine to not have to decide what to wear each day or dig through their closets and dresser drawers to see what colors go with what. Changing colors and styles of dress is a social custom, one that is more important when one goes out than when one stays at home. Styles and colors are often dictated by fashion and the desire to conform or not to conform. By opting out, perhaps Dickinson signaled unconsciously that she was not buying into this societal expectation that people change the styles and colors of their clothing on a daily basis. White was no doubt easier to mend as well, with no faded colors or designs that would not match newer swatches on repair. Maybe she saw white as dwelling in possibility, just like the clean white beginning of a fresh sheet of paper. Perhaps she chose white because she could accent in any way she pleased with color given her mood, perhaps with a blue shawl one day or the brown paisley shawl that is still on display at the Homestead the next. Or maybe the choice was a defensive one for more writing time—she could better avoid the housework she dreaded if Vinnie allowed her not to get her white dresses soiled. White day dresses, however, like the only remaining dress, were commonly worn for working indoors.

The point is that if Dickinson had some aesthetic or personal reason for wearing white frequently, if not exclusively sometime after the 1860s, she did not make that reason definitively known in her extant writing. Until more documentary evidence can be found, this will remain one of the poet's mysteries.

"THE WAR BETWEEN THE HOUSES"

Less a mystery but more a controversy and one that is more important to the reading and influence of the poet down through the years is actually a drama that scholars know quite a bit about. This is the problem that has come to be known as the "war between the houses." The war started when Austin began his affair with Mabel Loomis Todd after Gib's death in 1883, and Vinnie and Emily were apparently complicit in it. It is known that Austin and Mabel had their first and many later rendezvous in the Homestead. The argument goes that for this to happen, both Vinnie and Emily would have had to have known about it and not said or done anything toward Austin to make the unfaithfulness stop happening in their home. "Their" home, however, is actually an incorrect characterization of the Homestead. With both parents dead and the fact that Austin was now the male heir who owned both houses, neither sister actually owned the home they lived in and maintained with the help of Margaret Maher and the groundskeepers. The house was Austin's, and that may or may not have influenced the sisters' response to what the male owner of the house they lived in wanted to do with his time there. Susan knew about the affair, and could not have been pleased with Vinnie or Emily for allowing it to occur right next door, however much she may have understood what may or may not have been their feelings of helplessness or resignation to it.

The rift that may have started between Vinnie and Susan, especially (since Emily and Susan had been close for many years), grew after the poet died, when Vinnie turned to Susan to help her publish Emily's writing. Martha Nell Smith has argued that Susan did not delay publishing the poet's work as has been claimed but that she struggled with her own grief over the loss of Emily while at the same time working on the poems and letters in a way that would create a publication that would honor the state in which they were found. That is, Susan wanted to present them artistically—more as a unique portfolio of mixed genres rather than changing them to conform to the popular conventions of print. Susan was a published writer herself and had offered criticism that was accepted and utilized by the poet in one of her best-known poems. Susan, of anyone, could probably understand most what the poet was doing with her manuscript books. She sought a way to present them to the world that would do justice to Dickinson's poetic project. As she worked, she was also under the pressure of having a flagrantly unfaithful husband and of having lost her youngest son just three years before. To top it off, now gone was her beloved friend whom she had corresponded with, shared books and writing with, and had lived beside as a member of the family for 30 years. Susan was working consistently on the manuscripts, but too slowly to please Vinnie, who was eager to see the poems in print. Vinnie took the poems and letters back from Susan and turned them over to Mabel Loomis Todd to help her publish them. If the feeling between the houses was a rift up to this point, this new offense propelled the war into full gear.

Todd took the opportunity and capitalized on it, some say using Dickinson to fuel her own ambitions and desire for fame. She enlisted the help of Thomas Wentworth Higginson, and together they had the first edition of poems out by November of 1890, just a little over four years after the poet's death. Susan's input was apparently neither solicited nor given for the first edition after her earlier attempt at editing them. Her voice was silenced not only in the way the poems and letters were presented (which were in conventional print with very heavy editing that changed their character and uniqueness almost completely) but also in her role in Emily's life. Written accounts of Sue that come from Todd are replete with scorn and disdain of her lover, Austin's, cold-hearted, nagging wife. Since Todd's biased version was the one that reached print earliest and was widely distributed and has expanded through other books down through the years, it is the picture of Susan Dickinson still held by many people even to this day.

Susan's importance to the poet as an early critic and mentor and lifelong friend and adult family member is only recently being studied more completely with the opening of The Evergreens to scholars. Also available are the materials in the relatively new Martha Dickinson Bianchi Collection at Brown University. Much of this material by Austin's wife and children has never been published, and it has taken until the twenty-first century to begin to be uncovered, studied, pieced together, and prepared for publication. Among the projects forthcoming from this material are a full-length biography of Susan Dickinson, an online critical edition of Ned's papers, the editing and publication of Martha Dickinson Bianchi's memoir, and a study of the poet's relationship with her niece and nephews, among other endeavors.

The war between the houses actually got worse than the bout between Mabel and Sue over the first editions of the poems. It extended over two more distinct phases. There was a dispute between Vinnie and Mabel over a plot of Dickinson land that Austin supposedly gave Todd for her work on the poems. After Austin died, Vinnie wanted the land and sued Todd to get it. In the meantime, she asked for the return of the manuscripts, which were still in Todd's possession. Todd refused and locked away several manuscripts that had not yet been published in any form. The poet had written so much material that her work was actually spread between these two parties. As it was, both sides had a considerable number of papers but neither one had all of them. Vinnie won the lawsuit gaining ownership of the land, but Mabel's daughter, Millicent Todd Bingham, later succeeded in publishing the papers that her mother had in her possession.

The next phase, or battle, of the war came after Susan, Vinnie, and Mabel were all dead. Susan's and Mabel's daughters, Martha Dickinson Bianchi and Millicent Todd Bingham, also published poems and letters that were in their family's possession. However, they did not cooperate with one another concerning the materials they had. As each of them was approached by interested researchers and each cooperated with different scholars about the information they knew, two respective camps began to form in the early scholarship about the poet. Some say the two camps are still firmly entrenched. Others argue that the schism is dissipating now that the youngest generation who knew any of the players is also passing on.

Despite issues over territory and bias that may remain, the most important concerns are still the ones Susan must have had in her mind when she looked over the large cache of manuscripts that Vinnie brought to her at The Evergreens in the early days after Emily's death. The question must have arisen: How should Dickinson's work—which she never prepared herself for publication and that is full of word variants, small sketches, letters that are also poems—best be displayed and shared with an audience who was perhaps never meant to see it in the first place?

THE SCISSORED VOICE

In *Rowing in Eden: Rereading Emily Dickinson*, Martha Nell Smith points out that there are several mutilations and scissorings in Emily Dickinson's letters.[1] When she began studying these deletions she found that they included cut-out portions of letters, passages crossed out in heavy ink, and erasures. Smith observed that most, if not all, of these deletions occur in instances where Emily is writing to or about Susan Gilbert Dickinson. Since the documents have been under the protection of various university libraries for decades, the only mutilations that occurred had to have been made in the years soon after Emily's death, and most probably were made by people who knew her or Susan or both. Through careful documentation, Smith develops a hypothesis that Emily's voice was systematically censored in her extant papers, probably by her brother Austin and his mistress, Mabel Loomis Todd, who served as the first editor of the published letters. The theory goes that Austin and Mabel manipulated the record left behind in Emily's papers to downplay the importance Susan had in Emily's life, either for their own satisfaction in demeaning Susan or as a protective measure for Emily's legacy in some way, or both. In terms of protecting her legacy, there is a suggestion that Emily loved Susan in a way additionally to friendship, sisterhood, or as a colleague of letters. Following Smith's argument and others, the excisions could have been made, particularly by Austin, to prevent speculation or embarrassment over the poet's sexuality.

Whatever the reason, the excisions and erasures in the papers do exist and are generally agreed to have not been made by Dickinson herself. Just as Susan Dickinson's voice was silenced in the record for years based on Mabel Loomis Todd's work on editing the first editions of the poems and lectures she gave about the poet, so too has Emily's been censored, even more graphically, with the active scissoring out of passages that were not to the liking of the censor. While the original writing underneath some of the cross outs and erasures may be pieced back together, other passages have been lost forever.

Other family members altered Dickinson's papers as well, perhaps with less malicious intent in mind. These include the Norcross cousins, Frances and Louise (Fanny and Loo), whom the poet loved so dearly. Both cousins believed her letters to them were private and should remain so. When Mabel Loomis Todd approached them for their letters to include in the volume she was editing for publication, both women mistrusted her and would not hand them over. Frustrated at what she saw as the cousins' blatant disregard for history, Todd kept pressing them for the letters. Finally, the cousins said they would be willing to copy over the letters in their own handwriting, omitting portions they thought too personal to be made public. Another silencing of the voice of Emily Dickinson occurred when, after making their copies, the cousins claimed they burned the originals.

It will never be certain whether Austin and the Norcross cousins did what they did to protect Dickinson's legacy out of the noblest of intentions or out of their own selfishness. However, they would seem to be among those who loved Emily best during her lifetime and would be thought to have kept her best interest at heart. The fact remains that their choice to make the decision over how she was perceived has silenced certain tones in Emily Dickinson's voice that can never be reclaimed.

THE DAGUERREOTYPE AND OTHER IMAGES

There are only four undisputed images of the poet so far in existence—two silhouette cutouts of the poet in profile, one as a young girl and one with her family while a student at Mount Holyoke; a painting by Otis A. Bullard of all three Dickinson children as siblings (the faces of whom all look the same), and the famous daguerreotype taken of the poet when she was 16 years old. Contrary to previous claims that the picture was taken at Mount Holyoke, more recent scholarship by Elizabeth Bernhard reveals that the picture was likely taken in Amherst sometime in 1847 before the poet left for college in the fall of that year.[2] Mrs. Dickinson also posed for the Daguerrian artist, William C. North, at the same time—the chair, table, and other props look the same in both portraits.

Not surprisingly, the poet did not like images, at least of herself, saying the "quick" wore off of them too soon. Rather than send Higginson one when he asked, she described herself in words instead, saying she was small like the wren, with hair the color of a chestnut bur and eyes the color of brandy a guest leaves in the glass. Vinnie didn't like the daguerreotype of her sister and commissioned an artist to try to soften it by adding curls and a ruffled collar. So began several doctored images. Ironically, at the same time the poems were being altered for publication and the letters scissored for posterity, the only authentic image of the poet was also undergoing heavy editing. According to Margaret Maher, were it not for her recovering the daguerreotype from disposal by the family early on, even this image would not be available.[3]

Over the years, claims to images of the poet have occasionally popped up. One of the most recent, the so-called Gura photo, was purchased by Professor Philip F. Gura for $500 from the Internet auction site, eBay. So far, scientific analysis can neither prove nor disprove the picture is a photo of Emily Dickinson. Manuscript forgeries, not atypical for any artist, have also been a problem in the past. A recent forgery was so well done that it even convinced many Dickinson experts that it was the real thing. Authentic new discoveries are rare, but they do happen from time to time. When they do, they elicit excitement and curiosity for what shade of light they may shed on unsolved mysteries concerning this poet.

NOTES

1. Smith, *Rowing*, pp. 11–50.
2. See Mary Elizabeth Kromer Bernhard, "Lost and Found: Emily Dickinson's Daguerreotypist," *New England Quarterly* 72 (December 1999): pp. 594–601.
3. See Mary Elizabeth Kromer Bernhard, review of *The World of Emily Dickinson*, by Polly Longsworth, *New England Quarterly* 64 (June 1991): pp. 332–34.

Chapter 12

"AN AMETHYST REMEMBRANCE": DICKINSON'S RECEPTION AND LEGACY

When the poet wrote to Thomas Wentworth Higginson in 1862 that publication was the furthest thing from her mind, that may or may not have been true. However, when she wrote that if fame belonged to her, she could not escape it, she was speaking a truth that even she could not have possibly imagined unfolding in the astonishing way that it has. Well over 100 years after her death, Emily Dickinson has not only not escaped the renown that most readers agree she is due because of the superior quality of her work, but she has also has not escaped the distortions of fame that she probably was well aware were possible. Perhaps she kept her Barefoot-Rank by self-publishing her work through hand-circulated letters to avoid the over handling of editors and the mistakes of print. In its best light, the poet's notoriety brings more readers to the poems, and it is the poems themselves, and the letters, that are her true gift to all. However, in addition to Dickinson's early reception, it is her influence on poets who came after her, and her persona in literary and popular culture that can provide three lenses through which observers may consider the poet's legacy.

EARLY RECEPTION

The first edition of Dickinson's poetry was *Poems by Emily Dickinson*, edited by Mabel Loomis Todd and Thomas Wentworth Higginson. It was published November 12, 1890, by Roberts Brothers of Boston. Its gray-and-white cover featured Todd's drawing of the rare and strange Indian pipes, which she had given to the poet a few years earlier. Todd hand copied and typed well over 700 Dickinson manuscript poems after Vinnie had brought them to her for help in getting them published. Emily's sister had grown impatient with Susan Dickinson's efforts toward publishing the works. From 1888 to November 1889, Todd transcribed the poems and arranged them into groupings of A-B-C, depending on her own view of their suitability for publication. From her groupings, Higginson chose 199 poems for the first publication, categorizing them into themes such as nature, love, time, eternity, and life. Among other changes, the editing included the addition of titles, modernized spelling, omitted dashes, changed line breaks and stanzas, and word substitutions.

Higginson first approached his own publisher, Houghton Mifflin of Boston, to see if they might be interested in publishing the poems, but they did not want to invest in the poems of an unknown poet. Since Roberts Brothers had published Dickinson's anonymous poem, "Success is counted sweetest," solicited by Helen Hunt Jackson in their *Masque of Poets* a few years earlier, they were the next publisher Higginson tried. Roberts Brothers agreed to produce a volume half the size of Higginson's proposal. They also wanted the poems edited to conform more to the poetry of the day. The publisher and editors compromised on 90 poems, but later Higginson and Todd managed to include a total of 116. Roberts Brothers agreed to publish an initial run of 500 copies.

Higginson's own essay, "An Open Portfolio," published in the *Christian Union* on September 25, 1890, did much to stir up interest before the new book of poems appeared. Besides providing samples of poems from the collection, it was here that Higginson put into print the familiar narrative of the poet's life as a recluse, one who rarely left home, and who wrote pure poetry as though it were for herself alone. He describes one poem as "woven out of the heart's own atoms" and describes her poetry in general as "poetry plucked up by the roots; ... earth ... stones.... and dew adhering."[1] As the coeditor of the first volume, Higginson's respected reputation as a man of letters and his active support of the project did much to instill expectations for Dickinson's debut in print.

The poems, even in their altered state, didn't need much publicity once they reached the shelves. The first volume was critically acclaimed by literary critics such as Robert Bridges and Louise Chandler Moulton. Influential writer William Dean Howells gave his approval in a piece in *Harper's Magazine* that compared Dickinson to renowned poets such as Ralph Waldo Emerson and William Blake. The first printing sold out within weeks, and the book went through 11 reprints in the first two years. The book was such a success that Roberts Brothers commissioned a second series of 192 new poems in 1891 with a green-and-white cover still featuring the Indian pipes, and a third series of 166 new poems in 1896 that featured a gray cover with the Indian pipes image.

Finding any first editions of the first three Dickinson volumes today is rare for a book collector or a Dickinson aficionado. In 2003, when the poet was beginning to be favorably compared with Shakespeare, a rare book dealer in New York City had an extremely rare listing of first editions of the 1890, 1891, and 1896 volumes available as a set in its catalog. According to the catalog description, only four copies of the first Dickinson book of poems had been available for purchase in the rare book collecting world in the entire preceding decade, and two of these had library stampings, which made them less attractive to collectors. The dealer's asking price for the set of three first editions was $15,500.

After the first three volumes of Dickinson's poems appeared in the 1890s, the manuscripts became divided between Vinnie and Mabel Todd due to their legal dispute over land; and two strains of publications, one from the Todd holdings of papers, and one from the Dickinson holdings began competing for readership.

It is worth noting that the reception of Dickinson's poetry has been, from the beginning, intertwined with her biography. Ever since Higginson's anticipatory articles in 1890, which set the mystique in motion for readers outside of Amherst, it has been difficult for readers to separate their readings of the poems from the image of the reclusive poet who wrote them. This fact both complicates and fascinates one's encounter with Dickinson's literary art, as well as her biography.

LITERARY INFLUENCE

Because of the changes her poetry has undergone in print, Dickinson's influence on other poets has seen an interesting evolution since the 1890s. While the early book publications enjoyed good sales and critical acclaim, the heavy editorial changes of the poems in them made them appear more conventional than they actually were. As Adrienne Rich has observed in her essay, "Vesuvius at Home,"[2] it was not until 1955 when Thomas H. Johnson edited a three-volume variorum edition of the poems, restoring Dickinson's dashes and other elements from the original manuscripts and printing them in what he deemed their chronological order, that poets began to take notice of Emily Dickinson as a new, authentic voice in American letters. That the early editions appeared so late in the nineteenth century and that the first variorum edition didn't appear until over 60 years later, made twentieth-century poets the first to really encounter Dickinson's work in full and benefit from her influence.

The 1890s did not see Dickinson's work ignored among writers of poetry and fiction, however. William Dean Howells, who had written an influential review of the 1890 *Poems*, found their unusual compositional style and subject matter of death and isolation appealing enough to recommend them to his friend, Stephen Crane. Facing the dawn of a new century, Howells found Dickinson's use of irony refreshing and appropriate for the times.

Early in the twentieth century, poets such as Amy Lowell, Edna St. Vincent Millay, Robert Frost, William Carlos Williams, and Hart Crane noted her influence on aspects of their work. For example, Lowell's 1925 poem, "The Sisters," acknowledges Dickinson as an older sister in American poetry. Lowell admired Dickinson's courage in deviating from exact rhyme and metrics, and was drawn especially to her use of imagery as a forerunner of the imagist movement. Lowell's appreciation influenced Edna St. Vincent Millay to also take Dickinson's work seriously as a model. Frost, who was not a native of the town but who taught in Amherst for many years, called Dickinson the best female writer in all of world history. He shared in her interest in writing about the New England countryside. While Williams Carlos Williams outwardly attributed more influence to Walt Whitman, the concision and imagery in his work shows the effect of Dickinson, whose poems he also admired.

In the mid-twentieth century, American poetry turned more toward an examination of one's state of mind, and Dickinson's work, which does this so prominently in poem after poem, became increasingly significant to working poets. Thomas H. Johnson's variorum edition of 1955, which restored the dashes and other idiosyncrasies of the poet's technique, changed the complexion of the poems from that moment on. As a result, Dickinson began to be recognized as an artist of the nineteenth century who was ahead of her time and who could perhaps be best appreciated by poets and readers from the twentieth century forward.

Robert Lowell's *Life Studies*, which employs introspection to the point of derangement, follows in the footsteps of much of Dickinson's work. Elizabeth Bishop questioned religion and other orthodoxies like her predecessor, and Theodore Roethke attributed several influences to her, including her riddles in concise stanzas, her spiritual questioning, and her boldness in exploring the unconscious over the rational. Beat poet Allen Ginsberg claimed Dickinson's influence early on in his work, and this is evident in his treatment of musicality in his early poems. Sylvia Plath's themes of the struggle between the creative life and the domestic life echo strains of Dickinson.

In the latter part of the twentieth century, when the women's movement reemerged for a second wave in American culture, feminist poets such as Adrienne Rich responded to Dickinson's treatment as a male-edited female poet of her time by writing not only bold poetry of her own that speaks to many of these issues but also writing essays that attempted to break Dickinson out of the female mythology that Rich believed had held her, and so many other creative women, back from full admission into the canon of great American literature. Rich was incensed by the wrong and unfair treatment Dickinson had received at the hands of her editors and other mythmakers. Her vocalized protest did much to rescue the canonization of Dickinson in American literature at a time when her work in its altered state may have been dismissed as ordinary or sentimental. As a result, she is now embraced as an artist who continued to struggle to find and keep her voice at a time that was exceptionally repressive for women—when they could neither own property nor vote. Contemporary poets such as Alice Fulton are attracted to Dickinson's puns, and influence from Dickinson is evident and acknowledged in the work of many other twenty-first-century working poets, particularly females such as Heather McHugh, Cynthia Hogue, Marilyn Nelson, and Susan Howe.

Due in part to late twentieth-century feminist scholarship and contemporary poets in particular, Dickinson's place in the canon of American literature was secured. Despite this, the distracting mythology surrounding the poet continues, and challenges to the relevance of her private work and fluid texts to a national literature go not completely unspoken.

THE DICKINSON PERSONA AND PUBLIC RESPONSE

Perhaps even the poet herself knew that she was creating a public persona in nineteenth-century Amherst. She may have realized that the smoke screen she was putting up between herself and others, whom she felt no desire to associate with, would help her maintain her fierce desire for privacy in a fairly public household. When visitors came to the Homestead and did not see her but instead received a flower or a poem on a tray delivered from her room, it is difficult to imagine that the poet did not realize she was adding to their already increasing curiosity. At the same time, the intensity of her work is so strong and prolonged that it suggests that the level of subconscious exploration she was engaged in perhaps just did not permit her to see herself as others would see her from the outside, or perhaps if she did, to care.

The poet once wrote to Thomas Wentworth Higginson that when she used the pronoun "I" in a poem she was speaking of a "supposed person."[3] This reminder to a professional editor that her poems should not always be read as autobiographical might also be applied to the Dickinson persona that developed in her own time and has been handed down over 100 years since. Who is this "supposed person" readers think they know as the poet? And moreover, how has her public image, or persona, been represented in popular culture over the years to the point of almost instant recognition, even among those who rarely read poetry? What has been the public response to the poet or her persona, particularly by those engaged in other artistic media?

Mabel Loomis Todd claimed that when she and David Todd arrived in town in 1881, for David to assume a professorship at Amherst College, the poet, now in her later years, was already known about town as the "myth." Despite her illicit affair with the poet's brother and their frequent meetings at the Homestead itself, Todd never met the poet face to face. However, she did play piano for her at the Homestead (Emily listened from upstairs) and the women exchanged a written note or two. Martha Dickinson Bianchi, the poet's only niece, writes that she and her siblings were discouraged from discussing their aunt with the town gossips. As facts became distorted and distortions multiplied and deepened, the woman and poet who was Emily Dickinson receded further into the background as a developing persona of her rushed out into the public sphere. If a social anxiety disorder, as Polly Longsworth claims, or some other kind of illness contributed to the development of this phenomenon, perhaps this "supposed person" is the result of one more device of the poet's to maintain her privacy.

Separate from Dickinson the woman and poet, the Dickinson public persona can be described as a reclusive, possibly agoraphobic, woman who *never* left her father's house (presumably her entire adulthood). The persona is a poetic genius who is so high strung that she flirts with moments of insanity on a fairly regular basis. She always wore white (again presumably her entire adult life), most probably in response to the jilting of a lover. In fact, the persona works best when she is seen as a victim of male dominance—she behaves as she does because of a father, a brother, a lover, her "Master," her minister, her God, and almost any other male figure one can think of. This public persona is intensely shy because she thinks that femininity means coyness, and it is attractive to males. The persona writes about home and prefers to spend her days there because she sincerely believes that is woman's place. The Dickinson persona refuses to publish because she would not dare to presume her poems would be worth reading by the public (and the public sphere should not be a woman's place in any case), and also because the first time they were sent out, the poems were rejected by a professional editor. The Dickinson persona's poems are creepy; they are preoccupied with death because of her morbid, depressed personality. This image of the poet does not laugh, and she does not smile, except perhaps in the occasional company of children. The image has strange mystical powers, however, which make her, in her vir-ginal white dress and chestnut hair tied up in a bun, not only capable of wielding power over others (males, in particular), but also prone to do so at unexpected and particularly poetic moments.

No matter how it first developed, the Dickinson public image is a fiction and a ghost manufactured out of half-truths and exaggeration. This ghost has haunted American mainstream and popular culture for many years and continues to do so. Unlike the tasteful celebration but nonetheless com-modification of her verses when quoted on greeting cards, stationery, book-marks, posters, pillows, magnets, and more, the abuse of Dickinson's image itself has become an industry all its own. This is one of the facets of the poet's legacy that has frustrated critics and scholars the most.

The Dickinson persona has been capitalized upon by everything from T-shirts to coffee mugs, from cheap cloth dolls to "brunch with Emily Dickin-son" at a Massachusetts country inn. As a result the poet's meek and creepy public image has been turned into a money-making enterprise. Dickinson images have appeared in television shows, where they are often ridiculed. The children's cartoon, *Hey, Arnold!* is an example from as recently as 2000. In one episode, a character cheats in a poetry contest by submitting a Dick-inson poem instead of her own original writing. She wins a trophy in the shape of the Dickinson image, complete with hair in a bun. The character then receives several messages throughout the rest of the episode from the ghostly figure in the shape of the poet emanating from the trophy. The mes-sages convince her to confess her crime. Although the moral against pla-giarism may be a good one for young people to hear in the popular media that is aimed at them, the objectification of Dickinson could hardly be more clear when depicted in the image of the ghostly trophy.

The image of Dickinson was placed on a U.S. postage stamp in 1971. Adapted from the daguerreotype by Bernard Fuchs, the stamp features a colorized image of the poet in front of a green background. Part of a series on American poets, the stamp provided the eight cents postage that it cost to mail a first-class letter at the time. The irony of Dickinson's image affixed to so many letters of those who never wrote to her is striking.

There have been well-intended artistic responses to Dickinson that have missed the mark as well, perhaps because they appeared as incarna-tions of contemporary biographical theories before more recent scholar-ship began peeling away the layers of the poet's mystique. These include dramas about the poet's life. One of the earliest of these was Susan Glaspell's 1931 *Alison's House*, which is considered to be a biographical treatment of the poet based on Genevieve Taggard's 1930 book *The Life and Mind of Emily Dickinson.* The play is characterized by its treatment of the recovered poems as a confessional about Alison's love of a married man. The play won the Pulitzer Prize in 1931.

In 1935, the play *Brittle Heaven* was written by Vincent York and based on the 1930 biography by Josephine Pollit, *Emily Dickinson: The Human Background of Her Poetry.* This play, like the biography, accounts for the behavior of its Dickinson persona by telling a tale involving the poet's supposed renunciation of Helen Fiske Hunt Jackson's future husband, Major Edward Hunt, so that Helen might marry him instead. Dorothy Gardner's 1945 *Eastward in Eden: The Love Story of Emily Dickinson,* dramatized the 1939 biography by George Frisbie Whicher, *This Was a Poet: A Critical Biography of Emily Dickinson.* In this scenario, the Dickinson image's strange behavior is explained by her star-crossed love affair with married Charles Wadsworth. Other dramatic renditions include Norman Rosten's 1969 play, *Come Slowly, Eden,* which disregards the historical facts even as they were known at the time when it portrays Higginson (who was not in fact present at the time) joining with Vinnie in poring through Dickinson's belongings and manuscripts after her death.

William Luce's 1976 play, *The Belle of Amherst,* which starred Julie Harris, remains the most well-known of the dramatic productions about the poet's, or her persona's, life. The play appeared on Broadway for 117 performances and won Harris a Tony award before it also played before millions on public television. Luce's version portrays Dickinson as a poet who rejects a normal life principally because of Higginson's early rejection of her poems. From the production of the play and the airing of the television special, generations of Americans formed their picture of who Emily Dickinson was. Many have seen the play more than once in its various revivals. The play drew attention to Dickinson at a time when new research into her life was occurring at an increased rate. It is unfortunate that the play, which drew such a wide and lasting audience, could not have benefited from the results of that scholarship in time to correct many of what are now generally agreed on by researchers to be misconceptions. A long way from *Belle* is the 1995 play *Emily Unplugged,* cowritten by Kate Nugent and K. D. Halpin of the Sleeveless Theater. The play is a feminist satire of the many critical and scholarly viewpoints that have appropriated the poet over the years.

Film responses have primarily been documentary and educational in nature rather than creative interpretations, and they did not begin to appear until the time of Luce's play. In general, these treatments have benefited from their documentary purpose and have been more successful in avoiding perpetuating a false image of the poet. Even in these later works, historical facts are still inaccurately portrayed. Early films include the 1976 *The World of Emily Dickinson*, starring Claire Bloom, and Jean Mc-Clure Mudge's 1977 production, *A Certain Slant of Light*, with Julie Harris as the host. In the former half-hour production, Bloom gives a stiff perfor-mance, and the emphasis of Vinnie's role in reading the poet's work in chorus with her is factually unlikely. Mudge's piece, by comparison, inserts fresher and more historically based influences such as that of Susan Dick-inson sharing books with the poet and responding to her work. The Dick-inson episode of the PBS documentary series *Voices and Visions*, produced in 1988, is one of the best cinematic treatments to date. Here, commen-tators as knowledgeable and varied as biographer Richard B. Sewall, poet and essayist Adrienne Rich, writer Joyce Carol Oates, and others begin to give a sense of the complexity of the actual life behind the persona. The readings of the poems by actress and narrator Jane Alexander voiced over images from the Homestead, cemeteries, and nature are effective. One of the most recent cinematic treatments is Jim Wolpaw's 2002 *Loaded Gun: Life, Death, and Dickinson*, which is a documentary about the difficulties of portraying the Dickinson image in film, and by extension, in any other medium. Becoming a film about making itself, the documentary takes a light-hearted view of casting the perfect actress to portray the poet. It also struggles with what cinematic approach (Hollywood or academic) to use, and what all of these choices can possibly mean when the Dickinson the director wants to portray continually eludes his grasp and understanding. In framing the film with a dream sequence of a Dickinson persona in the absurd position of stepping across a dusty baseball field ready to play hard-ball, Wolpaw effectively depicts the absurdity of the enterprise of convey-ing Dickinson's image in film. At the same time in his efforts to do so, he successfully captures the power contained in her words alone.

Indeed, the most tasteful public and artistic responses to the poet and their results avoid the false persona to a large degree and instead privilege the words of the poems and letters themselves. For example, Dickinson is quoted in award-winning films such as *Sophie's Choice* and Jane Campion's *The Piano*. Genius dancer and choreographer Martha Graham's 1940 *Let-ter to the World* depicts the poet in a struggle between a life of love (dance) and a solitary one of words (stillness). After a series of movements depict-ing various stages of the poet's life and shifting personae that develop the various struggles, the dance resolves when the poet resigns herself to the strength and lure of her own words, and to living alone as a poet. Con-temporary painter, sculptor, and performance artist Lesley Dill focuses on the interplay between Dickinson's words and parts of the body. She incor-porates one image from the Dickinson persona, the white dress, in a multitude of ways. One of these is *White Poem Dress*, a 1993 sculpture of painted metal and plaster of a tall and round white dress, standing on its own, unoccupied and cut through with words from a Dickinson poem, "This World is not Conclusion" in various sizes and shapes. Another interpretation by Dill uses the dress image (rather than a focus on a persona of the poet in the dress) in a performance piece of a Dickinson poem where the artist wears a large white dress, is "wounded," and "bleeds." The "bleeding" is portrayed by the pulling out of the dress of many seemingly endless strips of red cloth while the artist remains suffering interminably inside.

Musical interpretations have also embraced Emily Dickinson. These frequently focus on the persona of the love-lost poet but also refreshingly focus on the intense internal world of her language as well. Classical and art song settings by Aaron Copland, Ernst Bacon, Leo Smit, and Lori Laitman join folk musicians like Sean Vernon and rock music composers such as Sebastian Lockwood in interpreting Dickinson poetry in musical form. Carlton Lowenberg's 1993 *Musicians Wrestle Everywhere: Emily Dickinson and Music*, contains a bibliography of over 1,600 musical settings of Dickinson poems, or almost as many settings as there are extant poems. The Emily Dickinson Music Society that was organized in 2002, claims there are many more settings than these in existence with more on the way.

Perhaps other poets are best equipped to interpret and respond to the conflict between the poet and her public persona. Since all writers must work at least part of the day in solitude, there is an inherent understanding among them that this poet has been mistreated in myriad ways by those attempting to discover who she is. They know the poet's true identity is in her work and have expressed this belief in their own poems. Others seek the poet based solely on knowledge of her from popular culture. A sampling of poems written specifically about the poet or including Dickinson in major ways include: "To Emily Dickinson" by Hart Crane; "Altitudes," by Richard Wilbur; "Your Birthday in Wisconsin You Are 140," by John Berryman; "I am in danger—sir—," by Adrienne Rich; "Amherst," by Amy Clampitt; "Emily's Bread," by Sandra M. Gilbert; "Emily's Mom," by Thomas Lux; "Reading Room," by Mary Jo Salter; "Taking Off Emily Dickinson's Clothes," by Billy Collins; "Two Ghosts," by Robert Francis; "Wonder Bread," by Alice Fulton; "The Impossible Marriage," by Donald Hall; "The Deconstruction of Emily Dickinson," by Galway Kinnell; "Emily Dickinson's Writing Table in Her Bedroom at the Homestead, Amherst, Mass.," by Sharon Olds; "After the Poetry Reading," by Maxine Kumin; "Frowning at Emily," by Alicia Suskin Ostriker; and many others. A recent anthology published in 2000, *Visiting Emily: Poems Inspired by the Life and Work of Emily Dickinson*, was edited by Sheila Coghill and Thom

Tammaro. It features 78 poems drawn from folders, which, according to the editors' introduction, were bulging with possible choices.

Books about the poet and her work continue to be published each year by biographers and critics, though both biography and criticism are still relatively new responses to her work when compared with literary figures of similar stature to Dickinson's. The first full-length literary critical treatment of the poems was *The Voice of the Poet: Aspects of Style in the Poetry of Emily Dickinson* by Brita Lindberg-Seyersted of Sweden, published in 1968. This book is still valued today for its insights into the reading of Dickinson's poems. The first full-length biography was written by the poet's niece, Martha Dickinson Bianchi, *The Life and Letters of Emily Dickinson,* and was published in 1924. Half of Bianchi's treatment is a memoir of the poet's life from her perspective as a member of the family. The other half contains published letters by the poet and restores Susan Dickinson's role in the poet's life and work. Susan's role underwent an early excision in Todd's public lectures following the publication of the first three series of poetry books.

DICKINSON'S CONTRIBUTION TO LITERATURE

Emily Dickinson's greatest legacy is contained, of course, in the writing she left behind. Her work is important not only in American literature but also in world literature. Even as her poems continue to endure the trial of translation around the world, international readers, critics, students, scholars, and academics increasingly discover and value her poems.[4] The Emily Dickinson International Society alone has chapters in locations as far-reaching as Saskatchewan, Canada; Japan; and Kiev in the Ukraine. *The Dickinson Electronic Archives* (http://www.emilydickinson. org) is in the process of publishing the poet's letters and poems (as well as family papers) on the Internet, making access to these materials free and universal to those with World Wide Web connection. Graduate students in China and elsewhere are writing dissertations on the poet, corresponding with American scholars about books and other resource material not yet available in their countries. As more and more readers become familiar with the poet's work, Dickinson's private portfolio, kept in the bottom drawer of her cherry bureau and perhaps in Irish maid Margaret Maher's trunk, expands, quite ironically, to reach the far corners of the globe. The work of this most private of poets appeals to the largest audience ever available before in the world.

What do readers find appealing about these poems, and what is their contribution to literature as a whole? Certainly most general readers are first drawn by the universal subjects of the poems—nature, death, immortality, love, and other themes. Many of them have an effect of consolation on those suffering from pain and grief as well, since Dickinson wrote out of these feelings herself and wrote and sent many of her poems to family and friends for this purpose. The intelligence and concision of the poetry drives its power—no other writer, except perhaps the best haiku poets of Japan, has managed to encapsulate so much depth of feeling and layers of meaning into so little a space with so few words. Dickinson's poetry surprises, as well. When a reader expects an exact rhyme, the poet uses slant rhyme; when the reader thinks he or she knows the referent of a pronoun such as *it*, the reader ends the poem and the mind is suddenly opened to several different possibilities for a referent—and none are definitive. These features enhance enjoyment of the poems and illustrate what Dickinson meant when the speaker of one of her poems says she dwells in possibility.

Other attributes of the poet's work that keep it front and center on the American and world literature stage as well as influencing the work of contemporary poets include the way the poems manage to combine the highly intellectual with the emotional; the poems' complex wordplay and gaming with form, syntax, and grammar; the use of the lyric, normally a very personal form of poetry, to consider larger epistemological and ontological issues; the way the poems subvert expectations, limitations, and categories such as gender; the relative ease with which the poems move from everyday, minute concerns to cosmic issues; and the near refusal of many of the poems to allow definitive resolution.[5] Today's poets still marvel at how Dickinson accomplishes what she did and at the multiple poetic skills she possessed.

A common feature that readers who love the poems often agree on is that the poet *seems to be speaking only to me*. The personal connection readers feel, as though listening to one heart and mind speaking in solitude directly to their own, is perhaps the most appealing of the poet's legacies. It is this quality in the poems that causes readers to seek out the poet's biography while at the same time disbelieving much of what they find. Readers keep coming back to the sense that they alone know the real Emily Dickinson—and they do—through the "amethyst remembrance" of her poetry.

NOTES

1. Quoted in Buckingham, *Emily Dickinson's Reception,* p. 8.

2. Adrienne Rich, "Vesuvius at Home: The Power of Emily Dickinson," in *On Lies, Secrets, and Silence: Selected Prose 1966–1978* (New York: Norton, 1979), pp. 157–83.

3. Dickinson letter to Thomas Wentworth Higginson, July, 1862 (Dickinson, *Letters*, Johnson, ed., 3 vols.).

4. See Margaret H. Freeman, Gudrun Grabher, and Roland Hogenbüchle, eds., "'There's a certain Slant of light': Swedish, Finnish, Chinese, Japanese, Yiddish," *The Emily Dickinson Journal* 6, no. 2 (1997): pp. 38–72.

5. Susan McCabe, "Influence on Poets," in Eberwein, ed., *Emily Dickinson Encyclopedia*, p. 234

APPENDIX A

FAMILY TREE

NORCROSS

First Generation

Norcross, Joel (1776–1846)	Maternal grandfather
Norcross, Betsey Fay (1777–1829)	Maternal grandmother, deceased.
Norcross, Sarah Vaill (1788–1854)	Maternal step-grandmother

Second Generation

Norcross, Hiram (1800–1829)	Uncle, deceased.
Norcross, Austin (1802–1824)	Uncle, deceased.
Norcross, Emily (Dickinson) (1804–1882)	***Mother***
Norcross, William Otis (1806–1863)	Uncle
Norcross, Eli (1809–1811)	Uncle, deceased.
Norcross, Lavinia (Norcross) (1812–1860)	Aunt
Norcross, Alfred (1815–1888)	Uncle
Norcross, Nancy Fay (1818–1824)	Aunt, deceased.
Norcross, Joel Warren (1821–1900)	Uncle

Third Generation

(Among many others)

Norcross, Lavinia (1837–1842)	Cousin by Aunt Lavinia, died at 5
Norcross, Louisa (1842–1919)	Cousin by Aunt Lavinia, "Loo"
Norcross, Frances Lavinia (1847–1896)	Cousin by Aunt Lavinia, "Fanny"
Norcross, Emily Lavinia (1828–1852)	Cousin by Uncle Hiram

DICKINSON

First Generation

Dickinson, Samuel Fowler (1775–1838)	Paternal grandfather
Dickinson, Lucretia Gunn (1775–1840)	Paternal grandmother

Second Generation

Dickinson, Edward (1803–1874)	*Father*
Dickinson, William (1804–1887)	Uncle
Dickinson, Lucretia (1806–1885)	Aunt
Dickinson, Mary (1809–1852)	Aunt
Dickinson, Samuel Fowler, Jr. (1811–?)	Uncle
Dickinson, Catharine (1814–1895)	Aunt
Dickinson, Timothy (1816–?)	Uncle
Dickinson, Frederick (1819–?)	Uncle
Dickinson, Elizabeth (1823–1886)	Aunt

Third Generation

(Among many others)

Dickinson, William Austin (1829–1895)	*Brother*
DICKINSON, EMILY ELIZABETH (1830–1886)	**THE POET**
Dickinson, Lavinia Norcross (1833–1899)	*Sister*

Newman, Clarissa (Clara) B.   Orphaned Cousin, by Aunt Mary
  (1844–1920)
Newman, Anna Dodge (1846–1887) Orphaned Cousin, by Aunt Mary

Fourth Generation

Dickinson, Edward (Ned)   Nephew
  (1861–1898)
Dickinson, Martha (Mattie)   Niece
  Gilbert (1866–1943)
Dickinson, Thomas Gilbert (Gib) Nephew
  (1875–1883)

APPENDIX B

LIST OF POEMS PUBLISHED IN THE POET'S LIFETIME

"Magnum bonum," valentine, Amherst College *Indicator*, February 1850.

"Sic transit Gloria mund," *Springfield Republican*, February 20, 1852.

"Nobody knows this little Rose - ," *Springfield Republican*, 1858.

"I taste a liquor never brewed - ," *Springfield Republican*, May 1861.

"Safe in their Alabaster Chambers," *Springfield Republican*, March 1, 1862.

"Flowers - Well - if anybody," *Drum Beat*, March 2, 1864; also *Springfield Republican* and *Boston Post*.

"These are the days when Birds come back," *Drum Beat* under the title "October," March 11, 1864.

"Some keep the Sabbath going to church - ," *The Round Table* under the title "My Sabbath," March 12, 1864.

"Blazing in Gold - and", *Drum Beat* and *Springfield Republican*, March 30, 1864.

"Success is counted sweetest," *Brooklyn Daily Union*, 1864; also later, in *A Masque of Poets* edited by Helen Fiske Hunt Jackson in 1878.

"A narrow Fellow in / the grass," *Springfield Republican* under the title "The Snake," February 14, 1866.

APPENDIX C

INDEX OF FIRST LINES OF DICKINSON POEMS

APPENDIX D

SELECTED READING OF EMILY DICKINSON

Among many other works and periodicals, Dickinson mentions the titles below in her letters or they are alluded to in her poems. Other titles are noted in family papers or collections with notations that suggest the poet read them; still others are among the textbooks used in the classes the poet attended at school.

Aeneid, Virgil
Antony and Cleopatra, William Shakespeare
Arabian Nights
The Atlantic Monthly magazine
Aurora Leigh, Elizabeth Barrett Browning
King James Bible
Called Back, Hugh Conway
Cape Cod, Henry David Thoreau
A Christmas Carol, Charles Dickens
Complete Concordance to Shakespeare
David Copperfield, Charles Dickens
Dictionary of American English (her "lexicon" companion), 1844
  printing of 1841 edition, Noah Webster
Dream Life: A Fable of the Seasons, Ik Marvel (pseud. of Donald
  Grant Mitchell)
Elementary Geology, Edward Hitchcock
Elements of Mental Philosophy, Thomas Cogswell Upham
Ellen Middleton, Lady Georgiana Fullerton

Emily Brontë, Agnes Mary F. Robinson
Essay on Man, Alexander Pope
Familiar Lectures on Botany, Almira Hart Lincoln Phelps
George Eliot, Mathilde Blind
The Head of the Family, Dinah Craik
The House on the Rock, Matilda Anne MacKarness
The House of the Seven Gables, Nathaniel Hawthorne
The Improvement of the Mind, Isaac Watts
Jane Eyre, Charlotte Brontë (at the time, printed under the pseud.
    Currer Bell)
Kavanagh, Henry Wadsworth Longfellow
The Last Leaf from Sunny Side, Elizabeth Stuart Phelps
Little Women, Louisa May Alcott
Manual of Botany, for North America, Amos Eaton
Night Thoughts, Edward Young
Of the Imitation of Christ, Thomas a Kempis
Old Curiosity Shop, Charles Dickens
Olive, Dinah Craik
"Only," Matilda Anne MacKarness
Othello, William Shakespeare
Paradise Lost, Milton
Parley's Magazine
Picciola, X. B. Saintine
Poems, Oliver Wendall Holmes
Poems, Ralph Waldo Emerson
A Practical System of Rhetoric, Samuel Phillips Newman
"The Rainy Day," Henry Wadsworth Longfellow
Religious Lectures on Peculiar Phenomena in the Four Seasons, Edward
    Hitchcock
Reveries of a Bachelor, Ik Marvel (pseud. of Donald Grant Mitchell)
Sabbath School Visiter
Springfield Republican
The Task, William Cowper
Villette, Charlotte Brontë
"A Vision of Poets," Elizabeth Barrett Browning
Walden, Henry David Thoreau

APPENDIX E

IMPORTANT PLACES AND HOLDINGS IN DICKINSON STUDIES

The Emily Dickinson Museum: The Homestead and The Evergreens
280 Main Street
Amherst, MA 01002
Phone: (413) 542-8161
Web site: http://www.emilydickinsonmuseum.org

Amherst College
P.O. Box 5000
Amherst, MA 01002-5000
Phone: (413) 542-2299
Web site: http://www.amherst.edu

The Jones Library
43 Amity Street
Amherst, MA 01002
(413) 256-4090
Web site: http://www.joneslibrary.org/

Houghton Library
Harvard University
Cambridge, MA 02138
(617) 495-2441
Web site: http://hcl.harvard.edu/houghton/

John Hay Library
Brown University
20 Prospect Street, Box A
Providence, RI 02912
(401) 863-3723
Web site: http://www.brown.edu/Facilities/University_Library/libs/hay/

BIBLIOGRAPHY

COLLECTIONS OF EMILY DICKINSON

Bianchi, Martha Dickinson. *Emily Dickinson Face to Face: Unpublished Letters with Notes and Reminiscences by Her Niece*. Boston: Houghton Mifflin, 1932.

———. *The Life and Letters of Emily Dickinson*. Boston: Houghton Mifflin, 1924.

Bingham, Millicent Todd, ed. *Emily Dickinson: A Revelation*. New York: Harper and Brothers, 1954.

Dickinson, Emily. *Bolts of Melody: New Poems by Emily Dickinson*. Ed. Mabel Loomis Todd and Millicent Todd Bingham. New York: Harper and Brothers, 1945.

———. *The Complete Poems of Emily Dickinson*. Ed. Martha Dickinson Bianchi. Boston: Little, Brown, 1924.

———. *The Complete Poems of Emily Dickinson*. Ed. Thomas H. Johnson. Boston: Little, Brown, 1960.

———. *The Dickinson Electronic Archives*. Ed. Martha Nell Smith et al. http://www.emilydickinson.org.

———. *Emily Dickinson's Letters to Dr. and Mrs. Josiah Gilbert Holland*. Ed. Theodora Van Wagenen Ward. Cambridge: Harvard University Press, 1951.

———. *Emily Dickinson's Selected Letters*. Ed. Thomas H. Johnson. Cambridge: Harvard University Press, Belknap Press, 1986.

———. *Final Harvest: Emily Dickinson's Poems*. Ed. Thomas H. Johnson. Boston: Little, Brown, 1961.

———. *Further Poems of Emily Dickinson. Withheld from Publication by Her Sister Lavinia*. Ed. Martha Dickinson Bianchi and Alfred Leete Hampson. Boston: Little, Brown, 1929.

———. *A Letter*. Amherst, MA: Friends of Amherst College Library, 1992.

———. *Letters of Emily Dickinson*. Ed. Mabel Loomis Todd. 2 vols. Boston: Roberts Brothers, 1894.

———. *Letters of Emily Dickinson*. Ed. Mabel Loomis Todd. New York: Harper and Brothers, 1931.

———. *The Letters of Emily Dickinson*. Ed. Thomas H. Johnson and Theodora Ward. 3 vols. Cambridge: Harvard University Press, Belknap Press, 1958.

———. *The Manuscript Books of Emily Dickinson: A Facsimile*. Ed. R. W. Franklin, 2 vols. Cambridge: Harvard University Press, Belknap Press, 1981.

———. *The Master Letters of Emily Dickinson*. Ed. R. W. Franklin. Amherst, MA: Amherst College Press, 1986.

———. *New Poems of Emily Dickinson*. Ed. William H. Shurr, with Anna Dunlap and Emily Grey Shurr. Chapel Hill: University of North Carolina Press, 1983.

———. *Open Me Carefully: Emily Dickinson's Intimate Letters to Susan Huntington Dickinson*. Ed. Ellen Louise Hart and Martha Nell Smith. Ashfield, MA: Paris Press, 1998.

———. *Poems by Emily Dickinson*. Ed. Mabel Loomis Todd and T. W. Higginson. Boston: Roberts Brothers, 1890.

———. *Poems by Emily Dickinson: Second Series*. Ed. T. W. Higginson and Mabel Loomis Todd. Boston: Roberts Brothers, 1891.

———. *Poems by Emily Dickinson: Third Series*. Ed. Mabel Loomis Todd. Boston: Roberts Brothers, 1896.

———. *Poems by Emily Dickinson*. Ed. Martha Dickinson Bianchi and Alfred Leete Hampson. Boston: Little, Brown, 1937.

———. *The Poems of Emily Dickinson: Centenary Edition*. Ed. Martha Dickinson Bianchi and Alfred Leete Hampson. Boston: Little, Brown, 1930.

———. *The Poems of Emily Dickinson: Reading Edition*. Ed. R. W. Franklin. Cambridge: Harvard University Press, Belknap Press, 1999.

———. *Poems of Emily Dickinson, Variorum Edition*. 3 vols. Ed. R. W. Franklin. Cambridge, MA: Harvard University Press, Belknap Press, 1998.

———. *The Poems of Emily Dickinson including Variant Readings Critically Compared with all Known Manuscripts*. Ed. Thomas H. Johnson. 3 vols. Cambridge: Harvard University Press, Belknap Press, 1955.

———. *Poems for Youth*. Ed. Alfred Leete Hampson. Boston: Little, Brown, 1934.

———. *The Single Hound: Poems of a Lifetime*. Ed. Martha Dickinson Bianchi. Boston: Little, Brown, 1914.

———. *Unpublished Poems of Emily Dickinson*. Ed. Martha Dickinson Bianchi and Alfred Leete Hampson. Boston: Little, Brown, 1935.

PRIMARY AND SECONDARY WORKS

Ackmann, Martha. "The Matrilineage of Emily Dickinson." Ph.D. diss., University of Massachusetts, 1988.

Agrawal, Abha. *Emily Dickinson, Search for Self.* New Delhi: Young Asia Publications, 1977.

Alfrey, Shawn. *The Sublime of Intense Sociability: Emily Dickinson, H.D., and Gertrude Stein.* Lewisburg, PA: Bucknell University Press, 2000.

Anderson, Charles R. *Emily Dickinson's Poetry: Stairway of Surprise.* New York: Holt, Rinehart and Winston, 1960.

Barker, Wendy. *Lunacy of Light: Emily Dickinson and the Experience of Metaphor.* Carbondale: Southern Illinois University Press, 1987.

Benfy, Christopher. *Emily Dickinson: Lives of a Poet.* New York: Braziller, 1986.

———. *Emily Dickinson and the Problem of Others.* Amherst: University of Massachusetts Press, 1984.

Bennett, Paula. *Emily Dickinson: Woman Poet.* Iowa City: University of Iowa Press, 1990.

———. *My Life, a Loaded Gun: Female Creativity and Feminist Poetics.* Boston: Beacon Press, 1986.

Bernhard, Mary Elizabeth Kromer. "Portrait of a Family: Emily Dickinson's Norcross Connection." *New England Quarterly* 60 (1987): pp. 363–81.

Bingham, Millicent Todd. *Emily Dickinson's Home: Letters of Edward Dickinson and His Family.* New York: Harper and Brothers, 1955.

Blake, Caesar R., and Carlton F. Wells, eds. *The Recognition of Emily Dickinson: Selected Criticism Since 1890.* Ann Arbor: University of Michigan Press, 1964.

Bloom, Harold, ed. *Emily Dickinson: Modern Critical Views.* New York: Chelsea House, 1985.

———, ed. *Emily Dickinson.* Bloom's Biographical Critiques Series. New York: Chelsea House Publishing, 2002.

Boltwood, Ethel Stanwood. *American Samplers.* New York: Scribner's, 1973.

Brose, Nancy Harris, Juliana McGovern Dupre, Wendy Tocher Kohler, and Jean McClure Mudge. *Emily Dickinson: Profile of the Poet as Cook.* Amherst, MA: Hamilton Newall, 1976.

Buckingham, Willis, ed. *Emily Dickinson's Reception in the 1890s: A Documentary History.* Pittsburgh: University of Pittsburgh Press, 1989.

Budick, E. Miller. *Emily Dickinson and the Life of Language: A Study in Symbolic Poetics.* Baton Rouge: Louisiana State University Press, 1985.

Buell, Lawrence. *New England Literary Culture: From Revolution through Renaissance.* London: Cambridge University Press, 1986.

Burr, Zofia A. *Of Women, Poetry, and Power: Strategies of Address in Dickinson, Miles, Brooks, Lorde, and Angelou.* Chicago: University of Illinois Press, 2002.

Cady, Edwin H. and Louis J. Budd, eds. *On Dickinson: The Best from American Literature*. Durham, NC: Duke University Press, 1990.

Cameron, Sharon. *Choosing Not Choosing: Dickinson's Fascicles*. Chicago: University of Chicago Press, 1992.

———. *Lyric Time: Dickinson and the Limits of Genre*. Baltimore: Johns Hopkins University Press, 1979.

Capps, Jack L. *Emily Dickinson's Reading, 1836–1886*. Cambridge: Harvard University Press, 1966.

Carton, Evan. *The Rhetoric of American Romance: Dialectic and Identity in Emerson, Dickinson, Poe, and Hawthorne*. Baltimore: Johns Hopkins University Press, 1985.

Cody, John. *After Great Pain: The Inner Life of Emily Dickinson*. Cambridge: Harvard University Press, 1971.

Coghill, Sheila, and Thom Tammaro, eds. *Visiting Emily: Poems Inspired by the Life and Work of Emily Dickinson*. Iowa City: University of Iowa Press, 2000.

Conrad, Angela. *The Wayward Nun of Amherst: Emily Dickinson in the Medieval Women's Visionary Tradition*. New York: Garland Publishing, 2000.

Crumbley, Paul. *Inflections of the Pen: Dash and Voice in Emily Dickinson*. Lexington: University Press of Kentucky, 1997.

Dandurand, Karen. "Another Dickinson Poem Published in Her Lifetime," *American Literature* 54 (1982): pp. 434–37.

———. "New Dickinson Civil War Publications." *American Literature* 56 (1984): pp. 17–27.

———. "Why Dickinson Did Not Publish." Ph.D. diss., Amherst, MA: University of Massachusetts, 1984.

Danly, Susan. *Language as Object: Emily Dickinson and Contemporary Art*. Amherst, MA: University of Massachusetts Press, 1997.

Davis, Thomas M. *Fourteen by Emily Dickinson, with Selected Criticism*. Chicago: Scott, Foresman, 1964.

Dickenson, Donna. *Emily Dickinson*. Leamington Spa: Berg, 1985.

Dickie, Margaret. "Dickinson in Context." *American Literary History* 7 (1995): pp. 320–33.

———. *Lyric Contingencies: Emily Dickinson and Wallace Stevens*. Philadelphia: University of Pennsylvania Press, 1991.

Dickinson, Susan. "Annals of The Evergreens." *Writings by Susan Dickinson*, in eds., Martha Nell Smith et al. *Dickinson Electronic Archives*, http://www.iath.virginia.edu/dickinson/susan/tannals.html.

Diehl, Joanne Feit. *Dickinson and the Romantic Imagination*. Princeton, NJ: Princeton University Press, 1991.

———. *Women Poets and the American Sublime*. Bloomington: Indiana University Press, 1990.

Dobson, Joanne. *Dickinson and the Strategies of Reticence: The Woman Writer in Nineteenth-Century America*. Bloomington: Indiana University Press, 1989.

Doriani, Beth Maclay. *Emily Dickinson: Daughter of Prophecy*. Amherst, MA: University of Massachusetts Press, 1996.

Eberwein, Jane Donahue. *Dickinson: Strategies of Limitation*. Amherst, MA: University of Massachusetts Press, 1985.

Emerson, Ralph Waldo. "New Poetry," *The Dial* 1.2 (October 1840): pp. 221–32.

———. *Emerson's Prose and Poetry*. Eds. Joel Porte and Saundra Morris. New York: W. W. Norton, 2001.

Erkkila, Betsy. *The Wicked Sisters: Women Poets, Literary History, and Discord*. New York: Oxford University Press, 1992.

Farr, Judith, ed. *Emily Dickinson: A Collection of Critical Essays*. Upper Saddle River, NJ: Prentice-Hall, 1996.

———. *The Passion of Emily Dickinson*. Cambridge: Harvard University Press, 1992.

Farr, Judith with Louise Carter. *The Gardens of Emily Dickinson*. Cambridge, MA: Harvard University Press, 2004.

Fast, Robin Riley, and Christine Mack Gordon, eds. *Approaches to Teaching Dickinson's Poetry*. New York: MLA, 1989.

Ferlazzo, Paul J., ed. *Critical Essays on Emily Dickinson*. Boston: G. K. Hall, 1984.

———. *Emily Dickinson*. Boston: Twayne, 1976.

Ford, Thomas W. *Heaven Beguiles the Tired: Death in the Poetry of Emily Dickinson*. Tuscaloosa: University of Alabama Press, 1966.

Franklin, Ralph W. *The Editing of Emily Dickinson: A Reconsideration*. Madison: University of Wisconsin Press, 1967.

Freeman, Margaret H., Gudrun Grabher, and Roland Hogenbüchle, eds. "'There's a certain Slant of light': Swedish, Finnish, Chinese, Japanese, Yiddish." *The Emily Dickinson Journal* 6, no. 2 (1997): pp. 38–72.

Garbowsky, Maryanne M. *The House without the Door: A Study of Emily Dickinson and the Illness of Agoraphobia*. Rutherford, NJ: Associated University Presses, 1989.

Gelpi, Albert J. *Emily Dickinson: The Mind of the Poet*. Cambridge: Harvard University Press, 1965.

———. *The Tenth Muse: The Psyche of the American Poet*. London: Cambridge University Press, 1991.

Gilbert, Sandra M., and Susan Gubar. *The Madwoman in the Attic: The Woman Writer and the Nineteenth-Century Literary Imagination*. New Haven: Yale University Press, 1979.

Grabher, Gundrun, Roland Hagenbüchle, and Cristanne Miller, eds. *The Emily Dickinson Handbook*. Amherst, MA: University of Massachusetts Press, 1998.

Gray, Janet, ed. *She Wields a Pen: American Women Poets of the Nineteenth Century*. Iowa City: University of Iowa Press, 1997.

Griffith, Clark. *The Long Shadow: Emily Dickinson's Tragic Poetry*. Princeton, NJ: Princeton University Press, 1964.

Guthrie, James R. *Emily Dickinson's Vision: Illness and Identity in Her Poetry*. Gainesville, FL: University Press of Florida, 1998.

Habegger, Alfred. *"My Wars are Laid Away in Books": The Life of Emily Dickinson*. New York: Random House, 2002.

Heginbotham, Eleanor Elson. *Reading the Fascicles of Emily Dickinson: Dwelling in Possibilities*. Columbus, OH: Ohio State University Press, 2003.

Higgins, David. *Portrait of Emily Dickinson: The Poet and Her Prose*. New Brunswick, NJ: Rutgers University Press, 1967.

Higginson, Thomas Wentworth. "An Open Portfolio." *Christian Union* 42 (25 September 1890): pp. 392–93.

———. "Letter to a Young Contributor," *The Atlantic Monthly* 9, no. 4 (April 1862) pp. 26, 402–11.

Hitchcock, Edward. *Life of Mary Lyon*. Northampton, MA: Hopkins, Bridgman, 1852.

Howe, Susan. *The Birth-Mark: Unsettling the Wilderness in American Literary History*. Hanover, NH: University Press of New England, 1993.

———. *My Emily Dickinson*. Berkeley, CA: North Atlantic Books, 1985.

Jenkins, MacGregor. *Emily Dickinson: Friend and Neighbor*. Boston: Little, Brown, 1930.

Johnson, Greg. *Emily Dickinson: Perception and the Poet's Quest*. University, AL: University of Alabama Press, 1985.

Johnson, Tamara, ed. *Readings on Emily Dickinson*. Greenhaven Literary Companion to American Authors. San Diego, CA: Greenhaven Press, 1997.

Johnson, Thomas H. *Emily Dickinson: An Interpretive Biography*. Cambridge: Harvard University Press, Belknap Press, 1955.

Juhasz, Suzanne, ed. *Feminist Critics Read Emily Dickinson*. Bloomington: Indiana University Press, 1983.

———. *The Undiscovered Continent: Emily Dickinson and the Space of the Mind*. Bloomington: Indiana University Press, 1983.

Juhasz, Suzanne, Cristanne Miller, and Martha Nell Smith. *Comic Power in Emily Dickinson*. Austin: University of Texas Press, 1993.

Keller, Karl. *The Only Kangaroo among the Beauty: Emily Dickinson and America*. Baltimore: Johns Hopkins University Press, 1979.

Kher, Inder Nath. *The Landscape of Absence: Emily Dickinson's Poetry*. New Haven, CT: Yale University Press, 1974.

Kimpel, Ben. *Emily Dickinson as Philosopher*. New York: E. Mellen Press, 1981.

Kirkby, Joan. *Emily Dickinson. Women Writers Series*. London: Macmillan, 1991.

Knapp, Bettina L. *Emily Dickinson*. New York: Continuum, 1989.

Lambert, Robert Graham, Jr. *A Critical Study of Emily Dickinson's Letters: The Prose of a Poet*. Lewiston, NY: Mellen University Press, 1966, 1997.

———. *Emily Dickinson's Use of Anglo-American Legal Concepts and Vocabulary in Her Poetry*. Lewiston, NY: Edwin Mellen Press, 1997.

Lease, Benjamin. *Emily Dickinson's Readings of Men and Books: Sacred Soundings*. New York: St. Martin's Press, 1990.

Leder, Sharon, and Andrea Abbott. *The Language of Exclusion: The Poetry of Emily Dickinson and Christina Rossetti*. Westport, CT: Greenwood Press, 1987.

Leyda, Jay, ed. *The Years and Hours of Emily Dickinson*. 2 vols. New Haven, CT: Yale University Press, 1960.

Liebling, Jerome, Christopher Benfy, Polly Longsworth, and Barton Levy St. Armand. *The Dickinsons of Amherst*. Lebanon, NH: University Press of New England, 2001.

Lilliedahl, Ann Martha. *Emily Dickinson in Europe: Her Literary Reputation in Selected Countries*. Washington, DC: University of America, 1981.

Lindberg-Seyersted, Brita. *Emily Dickinson's Punctuation*. Oslo: American Institute, University of Oslo Press, 1976.

———. *The Voice of the Poet: Aspects of Style in the Poetry of Emily Dickinson*. Cambridge: Harvard University Press, 1968.

Loeffelholz, Mary. *Dickinson and the Boundaries of Feminist Theory*. Urbana: University of Illinois Press, 1991.

Lombardo, Daniel. *Hedge Away: The Other Side of Emily Dickinson's Amherst*. Northampton, MA: *Daily Hampshire Gazette*, 1997.

Longsworth, Polly. *Austin and Mabel: The Amherst Affair and Love Letters of Austin Dickinson and Mabel Loomis Todd*. New York: Farrar, Straus and Giroux, 1983.

———. *The World of Emily Dickinson*. New York: Norton, 1990.

Loving, Jerome. *Emily Dickinson: The Poet on the Second Story*. Cambridge: Cambridge University Press, 1986.

Lowell, Robert. *Life Studies*. New York: Farrar, Straus, and Cudahy, 1959.

Lowenberg, Carl. *Emily Dickinson's Textbooks*. Lafayette, CA: C. Lowenberg, 1986.

———. *Musicians Wrestle Everywhere: Emily Dickinson and Music*. Berkeley, CA: Fallen Leaf, 1992.

Lubbers, Klaus. *Emily Dickinson: The Critical Revolution*. Ann Arbor: University of Michigan Press, 1968.

Lucas, Dolores Dyer. *Emily Dickinson and Riddle*. DeKalb: Northern Illinois University Press, 1968.

Lundin, Roger. *Emily Dickinson and the Art of Belief*. Grand Rapids, MI: William B. Eerdmans Publishing Co., 1998.

Martin, Wendy. *An American Triptych: Anne Bradstreet, Emily Dickinson, Adrienne Rich*. Chapel Hill: University of North Carolina Press, 1984.

———, ed. *The Cambridge Companion to Emily Dickinson*. London: Cambridge University Press, 2002.

McCabe, Susan. "Influence on Poets." In *Emily Dickinson Encyclopedia*, ed. Jane Donahue Eberwein. Amherst, MA: University of Massachusetts Press, 1985.

McIntosh, James. *Nimble Believing: Dickinson and the Unknown*. Ann Arbor: University of Michigan Press, 2000.

McNaughton, Ruth F. *The Imagery of Emily Dickinson*. Folcroft, PA: Folcroft Library Editions, 1974.

McNeil, Helen. *Emily Dickinson*. London: Virago, 1986.

Messmer, Marietta. *A Vice for Voices: Reading Emily Dickinson's Correspondences*. Amherst, MA: University of Massachusetts Press, 2001.

Miller, Cristanne. *Emily Dickinson: A Poet's Grammar*. Cambridge, MA: Harvard University Press, 1987.

Miller, Ruth. *The Poetry of Emily Dickinson*. Middletown, CT: Wesleyan University Press, 1968.

Mitchell, Domhnall. *Emily Dickinson: Monarch of Perception*. Amherst, MA: University of Massachusetts Press, 2000.

More, Hannah. *Coelebs in Search of a Wife*. 8th ed. London: T. Cadell and W. Davies, 1809.

Mossberg, Barbara Antonina Clarke. *Emily Dickinson: When a Writer Is a Daughter*. Bloomington: Indiana University Press, 1982.

Mudge, Jean McClure. *Emily Dickinson and the Image of Home*. Amherst, MA: University of Massachusetts Press, 1975.

Murray, Aífe. "Miss Margaret's Emily Dickinson." *Signs: A Journal of Women in Culture and Society* 24, no. 3 (spring 1999): pp. 697–732.

Murray, Lindley. *An English Grammar: Comprehending the Principles and Rules of the Language*. Frankfort, KY: A. G. Hodges, printer, 1932.

Oberhaus, Dorothy Huff. *Emily Dickinson's Fascicles: Method and Meaning*. University Park: Pennsylvania State University Press, 1995.

Oliver, Virginia H. *Apocalypse of Greece: A Study of Emily Dickinson's Eschatology*. New York: Peter Lang, 1989.

Olney, James. *The Languages of Poetry: Walt Whitman, Emily Dickinson, Gerard Manley Hopkins*. Athens: University of Georgia Press, 1993.

Orzeck, Martin, and Robert Weisbuch, eds. *Dickinson and Audience*. Ann Arbor: University of Michigan Press, 1996.

Ottlinger, Claudia. *The Death-Motif in the Poetry of Emily Dickinson and Christina Rossetti*. New York: Peter Lang, 1996.

Patterson, Rebecca. *Emily Dickinson's Imagery*. Edited posthumously by Margaret H. Freeman. Amherst, MA: University of Massachusetts Press, 1979.

———. *The Riddle of Emily Dickinson*. Boston: Houghton Mifflin, 1951.

Petrino, Elizabeth. *Emily Dickinson and Her Contemporaries: Women's Verse in America, 1820–1885*. Hanover, NH: University Press of New England, 1998.

Phillips, Elizabeth. *Emily Dickinson: Personae and Performance*. University Park: Pennsylvania State University Press, 1988.

Pollack, Vivian R. *A Poet's Parents: The Courtship Letters of Emily Norcross and Edward Dickinson*. Chapel Hill: University of North Carolina Press, 1988.

———. *Dickinson: The Anxiety of Gender*. Ithaca, NY: Cornell University Press, 1984.

———, ed. *A Historical Guide to Emily Dickinson*. New York: Oxford University Press, 2004.

Pollitt, Josephine. *Emily Dickinson: The Human Background of Her Poetry*. New York: Harper, 1930.

Porter, David T. *The Art of Emily Dickinson's Early Poetry*. Cambridge, MA: Harvard University Press, 1966.

———. *Dickinson: The Modern Idiom*. Cambridge, MA: Harvard University Press, 1981.

Power, Mary James, Sister. *In the Name of the Bee: The Significance of Emily Dickinson*. New York: Sheed and Ward, 1943.

Pritchard, William H. *Talking Back to Emily Dickinson and Other Essays*. Amherst, MA: University of Massachusetts Press, 1998.

Reynolds, David S. *Beneath the American Renaissance: The Subversive Imagination in the Age of Emerson and Melville*, New York: Knopf, 1988.

Robinson, John. *Emily Dickinson: Looking to Canaan*. Boston: Faber and Faber, 1986.

Rupp, Richard H. *Critics on Emily Dickinson*. Miami, FL: University of Miami Press, 1972.

St. Armand, Barton Levi. *Emily Dickinson and Her Culture: The Soul's Society*. Cambridge: Cambridge University Press, 1984.

Salska, Agnieszka. *Walt Whitman and Emily Dickinson: Poetry of the Central Consciousness*. Philadelphia: University of Pennsylvania Press, 1985.

Sewall, Richard Benson, ed. *Emily Dickinson, a Collection of Critical Essays*. Englewood Cliffs, NJ: Prentice-Hall, 1963.

———. *The Life of Emily Dickinson*. 2 vols. New York: Farrar, Straus and Giroux, 1974.

———. *The Lyman Letters: New Light on Emily Dickinson and Her Family*. Amherst, MA: University of Massachusetts Press, 1965.

Sherwood, William. *Circumference and Circumstance: Stages in the Mind and Art of Emily Dickinson*. New York: Columbia University Press, 1968.

Shurr, William H. *The Marriage of Emily Dickinson: A Study of the Fascicles*. Lexington, KY: University Press of Kentucky, 1983.

Sielke, Sabine, ed. *Fashioning the Female Subject: The Intertextual Networking of Dickinson, Moore, and Rich*. Ann Arbor: University of Michigan Press, 1997.

Small, Judy Jo. *Positive as Sound: Emily Dickinson's Rhyme*. Athens: University of Georgia Press, 1990.

Smith, Martha Nell. *Rowing in Eden: Rereading Emily Dickinson*. Austin: University of Texas Press, 1992.

Smith, Robert McClure. *The Seductions of Emily Dickinson*. Tuscaloosa: University of Alabama Press, 1996.

Sohn, Youngmi. *The Challenge of Temporality: The Time Poems of Emily Dickinson*, New York: Peter Lang, 2000.

Stocks, Kenneth. *Emily Dickinson and the Modern Consciousness: A Poet of Our Time*. New York: St. Martin's Press, 1988.

Stonum, Gary Lee. *The Dickinson Sublime*. Madison: University of Wisconsin Press, 1990.

Strickland, Georgiana. "Emily Dickinson's Colorado." *Emily Dickinson Journal* 8, no. 1 (1999): pp. 1–23.

Taggard, Genevieve. *The Life and Mind of Emily Dickinson*. New York: Knopf, 1930.

Thackrey, Donald E. *Emily Dickinson's Approach to Poetry*. Lincoln: University of Nebraska, 1954.

Thoreau, Henry David. *Walden*. (1854). Princeton, NJ: Princeton University Press, 1989.

Thota, Anand Rao. *Emily Dickinson: The Metaphysical Tradition*. Atlantic Highlands, NJ: Humanities, 1982.

Tripp, Raymond P., Jr. *Duty, Body, and World in the Works of Emily Dickinson: Reorganizing the Estimate*. Lewiston, NY: Edwin Mellon Press, 2000.

———. *The Mysterious Kingdom of Emily Dickinson's Poetry*. Denver, CO: Society for New Language Study, 1988.

Uno, Hiroko. *Emily Dickinson Visits Boston*. Kyoto, Japan: Yamaguchi Publishing House, 1990.

Untermeyer, Louis, ed. *Emily Dickinson, 1830–1886*. New York: Simon and Schuster, 1927.

Walker, Cheryl. *The Nightingale's Burden: Women Poets and American Culture before 1900*. Bloomington: Indiana University Press, 1982.

Walsh, John Evangelist. *This Brief Tragedy: Unraveling the Todd-Dickinson Affair*. New York: C. Weidenfeld, 1991.

———. *The Hidden Life of Emily Dickinson*. New York: Simon and Schuster, 1971.

Ward, Bruce. *The Gift of Screws: The Poetic Strategies of Emily Dickinson*. Troy, NY: Whitson Publishing, 1994.

Ward, Theodora. *The Capsule of the Mind: Chapters in the Mind of Emily Dickinson*. Cambridge, MA: Harvard University Press, 1961.

Wardrop, Daneen. *Emily Dicknson's Gothic: Goblin with a Gauge*. Iowa City: University of Iowa Press, 1996.

Weisbuch, Robert. *Emily Dickinson's Poetry*. Chicago: University of Chicago Press, 1975.

Wells, Henry Willis. *Introduction to Emily Dickinson*. Chicago: Hendricks House, 1947.

Werner, Marta. *Emily Dickinson's Open Folios: Scenes of Reading, Surfaces of Writing*. Ann Arbor: University of Michigan Press, 1995.

Whicher, George Frisbie. *This Was a Poet: A Critical Biography of Emily Dickinson*. New York: Charles Scribner's Sons, 1938.

Wilson, Raymond Jackson. *Figures of Speech: American Writers and the Literary Marketplace: From Benjamin Franklin to Emily Dickinson*. New York: Knopf, 1989.

Wolff, Cynthia Griffin. *Emily Dickinson*. Reading, MA: Addison-Wesley, 1988.

Wolosky, Shira. *Emily Dickinson: A Voice of War*. New Haven, CT: Yale University Press, 1984.

Wylder, Edith. *The Last Face: Emily Dickinson's Manuscripts*. Albuquerque: University of New Mexico Press, 1971.

REFERENCE WORKS

Boswell, Jeanetta. *Emily Dickinson: A Bibliography of Secondary Sources, with Selective Annotations, 1890 through 1987*. Jefferson, NC: McFarland, 1989.

Buckingham, Willis J. *Emily Dickinson, an Annotated Bibliography: Writings, Scholarship, Criticism, and Ana, 1850–1968*. Bloomington: Indiana University Press, 1970.

Clendenning, Sheila T. *Emily Dickinson, A Bibliography, 1850–1967*. Kent: Kent State University Press, 1968.

Dandurand, Karen. *Dickinson Scholarship: An Annotated Bibliography, 1969–1985*. New York: Garland Publishing, 1988.

Duchac, Joseph. *The Poems of Emily Dickinson: An Annotated Guide to Commentary*. Boston: G.K. Hall, 1979.

Eberwein, Jane Donahue, ed. *An Emily Dickinson Encyclopedia*. Westport, CT: Greenwood Press, 1998.

Hampson, Alfred Leete. *Emily Dickinson: A Bibliography*. Northampton, MA: The Hampshire Bookshop, 1930.

168 BIBLIOGRAPHY

MacKenzie, Cynthia. *A Concordance to the Letters of Emily Dickinson*. Boulder: Colorado University Press, 2000.
Rosenbaum, Stanford P., ed. *A Concordance to the Poems of Emily Dickinson*. Ithaca, NY: Cornell University Press, 1964.
Webster, Noah. *An American Dictionary of the English Language*. New Haven, CT: N. Webster, 1841.

WEB SITES

Dickinson Electronic Archives: http://www.emilydickinson.org/
Emily Dickinson International Society: http://www.cwru.edu/affil/edis/edisindex.html
The Emily Dickinson Museum–The Homestead and The Evergreens: http://www.emilydickinsonmuseum.org

INDEX

About the Author

CONNIE ANN KIRK is a writer and scholar who specializes in children's literature, American literature, and Emily Dickinson. She teaches English at Mansfield University in Pennsylvania. She is author of *J. K. Rowling: A Biography* (Greenwood Press, 2004), and editor of Greenwood Press's forthcoming *Encyclopedia of American Children's and Young Adult Literature*. The author makes a donation from the proceeds of her Emily Dickinson biography to the Emily Dickinson Museum in Amherst, Massachusetts, toward the historical preservation of the Dickinson houses, The Homestead and The Evergreens.